"The book is great! There is no harder book in scripture to explain and extol than the Revelation to Saint John the Divine! It is a must-read for clergy! We are living in a time much like that which John faced, with uncertainties at every turn! . . . Reading Mother Meade's book might help many of us who avoid reading about difficult challenges in our own age! Go for it!"

—David Lowry, Rector Emeritus, Christ Church Cathedral, New Orleans

"Dr. Meade has given the world a tremendous gift. The Angers Tapestries are a testament to the shimmering artistry of the fourteenth century and there is no lover of art, of medieval Europe, or of the Christian Scriptures who will not find their horizons ripped wide open by this remarkable monograph. Dr. Meade's particular attention to the subtleties of the most unique and enigmatic book of Sacred Scripture allows the combination of staggering artistry and theological acumen behind these tapestries to shine forth. Highly recommended!"

—Matthew S. C. Olver, Senior Lecturer in Liturgics, Nashotah House Theological Seminary

"The Apocalypse tapestries in the Castle of Angers, France, form the largest collection of tapestries in the world and are a UNESCO World Heritage site. As a student at a lycée in Angers, I visited a number of times to contemplate the extraordinary images. Meade's introduction to the book itself is complete, well-researched, and uncontroversial. As guide to the tapestries, she weaves together both the medieval masterpieces and the text. It is a fresh new way to think about what John's vision was really about. Highly recommended."

—PIERRE WHALON, Retired Bishop, Convocation of Episcopal Churches in Europe

"The Angers Apocalypse is the world's largest surviving set of medieval tapestries and one of the greatest works of art inspired by the Bible's complex and arresting final book. Jean Meade's *The Last Word* breathes life into their threads through learned commentary, pastoral insight, and a commanding grasp of Western culture."

—MARK MICHAEL, editor-in-chief, *The Living Church*

The Last Word

The Last Word

*A Study of the "Revelation to John"
and the Fourteenth-Century Tapestries
of the Apocalypse of Angers, France*

JEAN ALDEN McCURDY MEADE

WIPF & STOCK · Eugene, Oregon

THE LAST WORD
A Study of the "Revelation to John" and the Fourteenth-Century Tapestries of the Apocalypse of Angers, France

Copyright © 2025 Jean Alden McCurdy Meade. All rights reserved. Except for brief quotations in critical publications or reviews, no part of this book may be reproduced in any manner without prior written permission from the publisher. Write: Permissions, Wipf and Stock Publishers, 199 W. 8th Ave., Suite 3, Eugene, OR 97401.

Wipf & Stock
An Imprint of Wipf and Stock Publishers
199 W. 8th Ave., Suite 3
Eugene, OR 97401

www.wipfandstock.com

PAPERBACK ISBN: 979-8-3852-4524-6
HARDCOVER ISBN: 979-8-3852-4525-3
EBOOK ISBN: 979-8-3852-4526-0

09/02/25

Unless otherwise indicated, all Scripture quotations are from the Revised Standard Version of the Bible, copyright © 1946, 1952, and 1971 National Council of the Churches of Christ in the United States of America. Used by permission. All rights reserved worldwide.

Scripture quotations marked (KJV) are from The Authorized (King James) Version. Rights in the Authorized Version in the United Kingdom are vested in the Crown. Reproduced by permission of the Crown's patentee, Cambridge University Press.

Contents

Acknowledgments | vii

Introduction | ix

1   The Seer and the Vision | 1

2   Revealing the Messages to Four Churches | 12

3   Revealing the Messages to Three More Churches | 17

4   Visions of God in Heaven | 21

5   Who Is Worthy to Open the Book? | 24

6   Opening the Seals | 28

7   The Interlude Before the Seventh Seal | 35

8   The Seventh Seal and the First Four Trumpets | 39

9   The Fifth and Sixth Trumpets | 46

10   The Little Scroll | 50

11   The Two Martyrs and the Seventh Trumpet | 53

12   The Woman Clothed with the Sun | 60

13   Satan's Accomplices: The Second and Third Beasts | 69

14   The Lamb on Mount Zion and His Worshipers | 81

15   Seven Angels and Seven Plagues | 92

16   The Seven Bowls Poured Out | 97

17   The Great Whore | 104

18   Visions of the Fall of Babylon: A Tale of Two Cities | 108

19   The Tale of Two Cities, or The Harlot and the Bride | 112

20 Satan and Christ | 118

21 The New Jerusalem, the Bride of Christ | 123

22 Come, Lord Jesus! | 130

Conclusion | 138

Bibliography | 141

Acknowledgments

THIS STUDY WAS ORIGINALLY inspired by a series of lectures given by the Reverend Canon John Fenton of Christ Church, Oxford, in the summer of 1985 as part of the Oxford Summer School in Religious Studies. Ever since then I have been a student and teacher of the "Revelation to John."

When I saw the tapestries of the Apocalypse at Angers, France, in 1992, I was amazed at their beauty and fidelity in making the fantastic vision of Revelation into a work of art like the stained glass of medieval churches, telling the story so even those who could not read the Scripture could learn and experience its message. The Caisse des Monuments Historiques de France was helpful in giving me additional access to them and in enabling me to purchase slides of the official photographs by Caroline Rose that appear in this publication. The beautiful book of these photographs of the tapestries, *La Tenture de l'Apocalypse d'Angers*, published in 1987 by L'Association pour le développement de l'Inventaire Général des Monuments et des Richesses Artistiques en Région des Pays de la Loire, is the source of much of my information about the tapestries and their history. I am grateful to my friend, Elroy Eckhardt, for printing and then digitizing these slides for publication in this book.

I am indebted to the *Interpreter's Bible* (Abingdon Press, 1957) with its side-by-side English text of the traditional King James Version and the original Revised Standard Version, and the introduction and exegesis by Martin Rist and the exposition by Lynn Harold Hough. I have also relied on the introduction to J. B. Phillip's translation (Bles, 1957) of Revelation and his observations about the Greek text. All English quotations from the Bible except those from Handel's *Messiah* are from the Revised Standard Version of the Bible, unless otherwise noted. The Greek New Testament which I have used is the 1975 publication of the American Bible Society, edited by Kurt Aland et al.

Introduction

THE NAME OF THE last book of the Christian Bible is "The Revelation to John." For some reason people always want to make that a plural and call it "Revelations," but it is singular. It is the record of one sustained ecstatic experience in which a man named John is granted a series of visions of "what must take place" in heaven and on earth. The Greek word for "revelation" is "*apocalypse*," and that word in English has come to be associated almost exclusively with this book and its visions of the final battles between good and evil which will precede the end of time.

Although this last book of the Christian Bible is not often read or preached upon in worship services, at least not in liturgical churches, it has held unparalleled fascination for generations of believers. While the strangeness of its language and its foreboding messages have made some mainstream theologians and preachers want to sidestep dealing with it, this book appeals especially to the artistic and mystical religious imagination. This testimony of a man who was granted a vision of heaven and an understanding thereby of God's purpose in the world has inspired many other literary works in the history of Christianity. The most famous of these is undoubtedly Dante's *The Divine Comedy*, written in Italy in the early fourteenth century, roughly contemporaneous with the tapestries from Angers that illustrate and illuminate this text.

The messages of this vision have also been deeply important to persecuted Christians in every age who need hope that their affliction will soon end and confidence that their trials have meaning and purpose in God's eyes. From the original audience of Christians in the Roman Empire at the end of the first century to the African slaves in the American South before the Civil War, to persecuted Christians in Indonesia, Africa, China, Pakistan and many other places today, those who fear for their lives yet hope to stay true to their faith have taken courage and inspiration from this book.

All of us who hope to be faithful Christians when our own trials come, and who pray in solidarity with those who are persecuted, find that the message of the book remains relevant and urgent.

WHO IS THIS MAN NAMED JOHN?

Who is this man who writes down his experience for his fellow Christians? He calls himself John; and the traditional answer is that he is John the disciple and evangelist, the brother of James, the son of Zebedee, whom they left alone in the boat when Jesus called the two brothers to come follow him. Let us look at some of the sources of what we know about the disciple and the evangelist, and consider the question of whether we have two Johns here or three, or whether they are one and the same person.

In the Gospel of John, the author refers to himself as "the disciple whom Jesus loved." Some scholars say that means the author is someone other than John the disciple—for example, Lazarus, whom Jesus raised from the dead. But the tradition is very strong that the author of the Gospel is John the son of Zebedee. Many biblical scholars, however, who believe that John the son of Zebedee did write the Fourth Gospel still hold that he was not the same John who wrote down this vision. They cite differences in the structure of the text, wording, and often confused Greek grammar in Revelation. J. B. Phillips, the noted twentieth-century translator of the New Testament, however, thinks that these differences can be explained by the form and intent of the text, which is a recounting of an ecstatic vision.

Furthermore, ancient ideas of authorship and of plagiarism were quite different from modern ones, and a disciple writing down teachings and experiences taught to him by a master often attributed the work to the master, not to himself. A disciple of John the disciple, writing down the things he had learned from his master, might well have attributed the writing to the original John. That is the accepted understanding, for example, of the second and third parts of the book of the prophet Isaiah in the Old Testament.

The tradition and heritage of the church, however, is a very important witness to authorship; and from the very beginning, they attributed these writings to one author, the beloved disciple, the brother of James, the son of Zebedee, one whom Jesus named a "son of thunder." According to this tradition, Irenaeus, the second-century bishop of Lyon, said that Polycarp, the bishop and martyr, had told him that John, the beloved disciple, whom he knew, was the author of the Fourth Gospel and the author of the letters

INTRODUCTION

of John and the Revelation to John.[1] Also, Eusebius writes in his *Ecclesiastical History* (ca. 310) that during the persecution of the Emperor Domitian in the last decade of the first century, the apostle and evangelist John was still alive and was condemned to live on the island of Patmos for preaching his Christian faith. In other words, the apostle, the author of the Fourth Gospel, and the author of the Revelation to John are all one and the same according to this first historian of the church. Eusebius also records the words of Justin Martyr that the Apocalypse of John was clearly the apostle's work. Origen wrote that although the second and third epistles may not be the work of the same man, surely the Gospel and the Revelation and the first epistle are.[2]

Since scholars in various fields of historical inquiry trust the authenticity of the oral tradition unless strong evidence can be found to the contrary, there are also many biblical scholars who accept the traditional authorship of Revelation as the work of the beloved disciple, John the son of Zebedee, at the end of a very long life. It can, in any case, surely enrich our appreciation for the book of Revelation to put it in the context of its traditional author. Although the anonymity of the writer does not necessarily diminish the authority of a sacred text, this book was included in the canon at least in part because early Christians believed it was written by John the beloved disciple. How needlessly impoverished we are if we assume the old tradition is false and say, "Who knows?"

For more understanding of the traditional author of this book, let us consider what we know about John from the rest of the New Testament. Three disciples, Peter, James, and John, are portrayed as Jesus's inner circle of friends in all the Gospel accounts; sometimes Simon Peter's brother Andrew joins them to make the inner circle two sets of brothers. It is Simon Peter, James, and John whom Jesus brings inside with him when he raises Jairus's daughter,[3] they are the only witnesses to the transfiguration,[4] and Jesus took these three with him into the garden of Gethsemane where they fell asleep while he prays in agony.[5] Jesus asks Peter and John to make the preparations for his last Passover meal.[6] John is usually thought to be "the

---

1. Cross, "St. Irenaeus's Testimony."
2. Origen, *Gospel of John* 5.3.
3. Mark 5:37, Luke 8:51.
4. Matt 17:1, Mark 9:2, Luke 9:28.
5. Matt 26:37, Mark 14:33.
6. Luke 22:8.

other disciple" who follows Jesus that night to the court of the high priest, the one who was known to the high priest and who spoke to the maid to let Peter in. He would then have been a witness to Peter's denials. On Easter morning it is only John and Simon Peter among the disciples who actually see the empty tomb. John runs there first but does not go in until after Peter does. His prominence among the twelve, then, is second only to Peter's. Just as Peter's leadership in the early church is recorded in the first part of Acts, and his epistles are included in the canon of the New Testament, the Epistles attributed to John are included. And then John's testimony to the vision granted him by the risen Christ is recorded in this last book.

It is interesting to compare the lives of John and his brother James as they lived out their calling as disciples of Jesus. They must have been very close, for when he appointed them to be among the twelve, Jesus gave them a name together: *Boanerges*, "Sons of Thunder." More often one thinks of the brashness of Simon "the Rock" Peter in the Gospel accounts, but this epithet given them by Jesus implies these two brothers were not shy or retiring either. In fact, the infamous dispute about greatness that arose among the disciples originated with James and John. They come forward and ask Jesus to grant that one of them can sit at his right hand and one at his left hand when he comes into his glory. In Mark's Gospel it is the brothers themselves who ask; in Matthew's Gospel it is their mother who makes that request of Jesus on behalf of her sons. (Certainly, following Jesus has become a family matter; she is a believer too even if her/their petition is misguided.) Whoever it is that asked, however, Jesus replies to James and John, "You do not know what you are asking. Are you able to drink the cup that I drink or to be baptized with the baptism with which I am baptized?" They reply that they are able, and Jesus tells them that, although they will surely drink of that cup someday, "to sit at my right hand or at my left is not mine to grant, but it is for those for whom it has been prepared."[7]

The cup that each was to drink was very different, humanly speaking. John is believed to have lived to extreme old age and been granted this vision at the end of a long life of witnessing to Christ. William Alexander Percy's poem "The Peace of God" captures the spirit of this long tradition about John:

> Young John who trimmed the flapping sail,
> homeless, in Patmos died.
> Peter, who hauled the teeming net,

---

7. Mark 10:38–40, Matt 20:22–23.

INTRODUCTION

head-down was crucified.[8]

James, however, was the first of the disciples to be martyred. In Acts 12:1–3, we read that "Herod the king laid violent hands upon some who belonged to the church. He killed James, the brother of John with the sword; and when he saw that it pleased the Jews, he proceeded to arrest Peter also." Herod, however, does not execute Peter immediately, and an angel of the Lord rescues him from prison. When John writes in Revelation about all the martyrs who have washed their robes in the blood of the Lamb, perhaps he is thinking especially of his beloved brother James and pondering the mystery of why James is killed while Peter is rescued, and why he himself survives them both to live a very long life.

This question sits at the heart of the biblical faith in God's love—love which is stronger than death. This love is constantly described as giving life and saving those who call upon God from death and destruction; yet God did not rescue James from Herod's prison. Moreover, we believe that in His infinite love for us sinners, He did not rescue his own Son from Herod and Pilate. "If he is the King of Israel, let him come down from the cross and we will believe in him,"[9] taunted the onlookers at the crucifixion; and that hypothetical "if-then" question rings out through history as the greatest challenge to the truth of Christianity, "a stumbling block to Jews and folly to Gentiles."[10]

The Revelation to John is an answer to this perennial problem of theodicy posed so long before by the psalmist: "LORD, how long shall the wicked triumph?"[11] Why do bad things happen to good people? Why do the chosen ones of God endure persecution, torture, and death? If God is in charge, why do those who defy Him succeed in getting and keeping power over those who follow Him? The Christian answer lies in the belief that God gives us free will to defy Him or to love Him, but that good will ultimately triumph in the end. In Christian theology, the Crucified One is the Chosen One; the resurrection vindicates him and demonstrates that fact to the world, including to those who put him to death. And in this vision, the Lamb That Was Slain now sits upon the throne for all eternity and will vindicate his faithful followers in the end. Furthermore, those who are martyred for their faith, following in the footsteps of their Lord, will be first

---

8. Percy, "They Cast Their Nets," stanza 3.
9. Matt 27:42.
10. 1 Cor 1:23.
11. Ps 94:3.

in the Kingdom of Heaven. That answer is set forth over and over again, in various ways that are strange, terrifying, or glorious, in this book.

THE SIGNIFICANCE OF BEING LAST

The Revelation to John is the last book of the Christian Bible; and there is significance to that place of honor which we should explore. Just as the book of Genesis, which means "beginning," is the first book of the Bible, telling the story of creation and the history of the patriarchs who heard God's voice, so the last book of the Bible foretells and describes the end, both time-wise and in the sense of *telos*, or purpose, of all creation and the destiny of the saints who follow Jesus. It is helpful to look at how the Testaments are organized to discover what meaning lies behind the placements of the various books. The Torah, the five books of Moses—Genesis, Exodus, Leviticus, Numbers, and Deuteronomy—are the holiest of all Hebrew texts. The rest of the Old Testament is comprised of the Prophets and the Writings, which are inspired but not of the same weight as the Torah.

The Christians who put together the New Testament were adding to the Old. They believed that Moses and the prophets had been fulfilled in the life and person of Jesus Christ, the son of David and the ultimate king of which many psalms speak. The four Gospels, which present the life and ministry of Jesus, are first in the New Testament to correspond to the five books of Moses. The Acts of the Apostles is next because it tells the story of the beginnings of the church, especially the careers of Saint Peter and Saint Paul. Then come the letters of Paul, some of which are the earliest texts we have in the New Testament, and the letters of Peter, John, James, Jude, and the anonymous letter to the Hebrews. Last of all there is this book, which claims to be a vision given directly from Jesus Christ to the author, a man named John, a vision which reveals the end of all things and of eternal life in Heaven.

Genesis tells the story of the beginning of all time, called *protology*, down through the history of the patriarchs Abraham, Isaac, Jacob, and his sons. The Gospels tell the story of Jesus who ushers in the beginning of the day of the Lord foretold by the Hebrew prophets. This last book tells the story of the end times, or *eschatology*, when the day of the Lord will finally come, and all things will find their fulfillment for which they were created. The "end" here has at least several layers of meaning: the final acts of the history begun on the day of creation, the revealing of the ultimate purpose of that creation, and the consummation of the will of God which has been working itself out throughout all time and within each human life since time began.

Amplifying the many parables of Jesus about the Kingdom of Heaven as a marriage feast or banquet, Revelation ends with the marriage supper of the Lamb, accompanied by songs and anthems of praise and thanksgiving. The hymns which John hears the saints and angels singing to God in Heaven have provided the texts for innumerable hymns, anthems, and spiritual songs throughout the history of the church. Most of our ideas and images of Heaven, moreover, are taken from this book as well, for in it the imagery of the teachings of Jesus, the Hebrew prophets, the Psalms, and the letters of Saint Paul all are brought together into a vision of eternity in the presence of God. It has inspired artists and writers and theologians through the centuries whenever their thoughts turn to describing life in the hereafter, as in C. S. Lewis's aphoristic statement, "Joy is the serious business of Heaven."[12] When Jesus said to the repentant thief on the cross, "This day you shall be with me in paradise,"[13] we are left with the question of what paradise is—what are we to expect? This book gives an answer.

SOME PROBLEMS WITH THE REVELATION TO JOHN

Although it is one of the most quoted books of the Bible, perhaps next to only the Gospels and the Psalms, Revelation is one of the most misunderstood and even maligned books of the canon. That is partly because of the use to which Christians have put the many prophecies and symbolic beasts which abound in the visions. Various groups or leaders have identified their political or theological enemies with the forces of Satan, as Martin Luther did with the pope. Various sects throughout the millennia have also tried to calculate the day that the Lord will come based on some interpretation of the days and years described in Revelation before the final victory of God. There have always been Christians who want to be able to explain every image and rationalize every poetic device to get a definite interpretation for each in order to obtain some arcane knowledge. For example, in 1996 Marshall Herff Applewhite, a man brought up in a devout Christian family, led his followers in the Heaven's Gate Community in California in a mass

---

12. Lewis, *Letters to Malcolm*, 93 (letter 17).
13. Luke 23:43.

suicide because he decided the "near" time described in this book was announced by the arrival of the Hale-Bopp Comet. That is just one example among many in the history of Christianity of people decoding the book of Revelation to explain current events and predict the end of the world.

Such use is misuse, in my view. Jesus said that even the angels in heaven do not know the hour or the day of his coming, so why would he have revealed it to his servant John in a vision, however cryptic? Obviously, he did not—to make such calculations is to miss the point of the revelation. It is a psychological necessity to think the end is coming soon for us to become concerned about it, so the visionary is proclaiming that the end is coming soon. It has become a staple of contemporary cartoons to have a figure of a bearded man in a long robe walking the streets with a sign saying, "The end is near." But the end is always very near for some of us, although we usually go about our business as if we had all the time in the world. The psalmist said, "Teach me to number my days so I may get a heart of wisdom,"[14] and Jesus told the parable of the rich fool who only thought about plans for a bigger barn, not knowing that his soul would be required of him that night. The visions of the end here are calculated, like that parable, to make us stop and think and listen to the word of the Lord about what really matters, what is really real and enduring. We are grievously mistaken if we think it is our buying and selling, our riches and power. This vision reminds us in every age that our real treasure is in heaven, where thieves do not break in and steal and moth and rust do not corrupt. It is a plea for us to set our hearts on that treasure and remember that, if the end is near, it means that our fulfillment is near. The longing of our hearts will soon be satisfied, for our Lord Jesus is returning as he promised.

And although scholars believe they have identified some of the sources for the various symbols and beasts based on current events at the time of the writing, if this book is to have relevance for Christians in every age, as the church leaders who included it in the canon surely believed it does, then the symbols must be multivalent; they must have meaning beyond topical references to contemporary figures and events, as interesting as it is to discover who and what these were. The beasts and the whore, the lake of fire and the pestilence, famine and warfare of the three horsemen actually describe the world as it was for those first-century Christians and as countless people throughout the two thousand years since and still today are experiencing it. The message is that there is an end to the suffering—it

---

14. Ps 90:12.

will come to an end soon, and moreover, there is a hidden purpose to it which will be revealed.

The Inevitability of Suffering

What puts some people off about Revelation, moreover, is just this clear teaching that there will be great suffering inflicted upon the whole world in advance of God's final triumph. We are very uncomfortable with any biblical teaching that speaks of fire and brimstone, the wrath of God, or of the devil or Satan. When such words are in the mouth of Jesus, we are embarrassed and try to explain them away as later additions by a redactor. With the book of Revelation, it is even easier for some Christians to dismiss difficult passages as topical references to arcane Jewish apocalyptic literature, about as important and interesting as parts of Daniel, Ezekiel, or Zechariah for serious students of biblical theology and history, but without much meaning for the person in the pew. Many Christians feel that the words of wrath and trials are not to be taken seriously as the actions of the loving Christian God. The fact that the messages to the seven churches which come from the mouth of Jesus in Revelation contain warnings and reproofs as well as commendations and promises, makes our modern sensibilities cringe. What preacher today could get away with saying such things to her or his congregation? The practice of convicting the congregation of sin before assuring them of God's forgiveness is only a memory for church history books in most Christian churches.

An Ecstatic Vision

Another difficulty with this book is that it is hard for many people in our day to believe in visions that are revelations from God. But the last book of the Bible claims to be just that and to speak with authority to all Christians, who should read and keep this prophecy. Does God really communicate with human beings that way, some might ask? Is the message from an ecstasy trustworthy? How do we know John did not just invent this vision as a literary device, like Dante did in writing the *Divine Comedy*? Another problem with a vision is that it seems less believable, less relevant, somehow, than if it purported to be history, like Acts, or advice, like Paul's letter to the Corinthians. Several of the books of the prophets in the Old Testament consist of series of visions, but this whole book is a vision. How important could the message of such a vision be to the life and faith of the church?

It is possible, however, to interpret the strange language of the book and the outlandish visions and apparitions as the attempt of a person who really has seen an ecstatic vision from God to somehow encapsulate it in writings with words that make sense before the dream fades away. Certainly, that is what the author is claiming to do; and that is the opinion, as we have seen, of the great translator J. B. Phillips. It certainly bears all the characteristics of an ecstatic vision: the scene constantly changes, as if in a dream, and the action does not always follow a logical progression, while statements in one chapter seem to be contradicted by those in another. When one tries to write down a dream, however vivid it may have been, words sometimes fail and logic escapes. The inconsistencies in John's account can be interpreted as just that—the inevitable result of trying to write down the vision and make it plain, and yet still be faithful to the experience that God had granted him.

The Nature of Kingship

Another problem that some Christians have historically had with this book is the emphasis on Jesus as the Kings of Kings; he is thus set above "the kings of the Earth," who are seen cavorting with the whore of Babylon. The kings of the earth are at last seen bowing down before the Kings of Kings, the Lamb upon his throne, so we can have hope for even the rich and powerful; but this book was not popular within monarchies because of the depiction of kings as anything but the right sort of leaders. When monarchs or their ministers had authority to select which texts of Scripture would be used in the liturgy in their countries, they did not choose Revelation very often. Elizabeth I of England is a ready example. When she forged her famous settlement to end the struggles between Catholic and Protestant factions in England, she had a strong hand in deciding what topics Anglican priests should address from the pulpit and what lessons they should read. The disuse of Revelation in the liturgy, once established, continued until modern times; the church of England did not normally read from Revelation in the lectionary except for the first and last chapters until revisions in 1966.

There is a story about George I of England hearing Handel's *Messiah* for the first time. When the "Hallelujah!" chorus rang out the text from Revelation, "King of Kings and Lord of Lords," the king rose to his feet, saying that he was only an earthly king. Everyone else immediately stood also, naturally. It became then the custom to stand at the beginning of the chorus, as the choir begins with "Hallelujah!" Evidently subsequent English monarchs did not continue to do so, however; only their loyal subjects persisted in the pious practice. The story goes that when the newly crowned Victoria went to her first performance of *Messiah*, she was told not to stand now that she was the queen. She remained seated during the first part of the chorus, but when "King of Kings" rang out, she stood anyway; and kings and queens of England have stood along with everybody else for that chorus ever since. Those words, and many others in Revelation, are stirring and even revolutionary if one takes them seriously.

Hierarchy or Martyrs?

Revelation also is not concerned with ecclesiology, so it was natural that the hierarchical church which developed in the West after Constantine did not want to emphasize it. There is no mention of bishops or priests as leaders of the faithful. The priority in the heavenly scenes is given to martyrs—ordinary faithful people who endure despite persecution. Naturally that did not endear this book to bishops, cardinals, or popes, who were the authorities behind the selection of texts for reading and preaching up until the Protestant Reformation of the sixteenth century. The only mention of priests, moreover, in Revelation is speaking of a kingdom of priests, much as Saint Peter speaks in his first epistle of all Christians as a "royal priesthood." But in Revelation it is only those who have been martyred for their faith who will come to life in the first resurrection when "they shall be priests of God and of Christ, and they shall reign with him a thousand years."[15] Such ideas blur the distinction between laity and clergy, so they did not gain prominence in church teaching; Martin Luther's doctrine of "the priesthood of all believers," which takes authority from this passage, was indeed revolutionary. But it also implies that to be a true priest, one has to be willing to suffer martyrdom, if not actually become a martyr. That's quite a high standard for any Christian, lay or ordained, in any time.

---

15. Rev 20:8.

INTRODUCTION

Fantastic Descriptions

And above all, the weird description of the beasts, the landscape, the people, and of Christ himself defy our senses as we try to imagine them literally. What theological teaching could be presented in such confusing and fantastic language?

It is helpful to recall, however, that this is essentially a Jewish-Christian book, in the tradition of the later prophetic works mentioned above. Jews were prohibited from making graven images by the second commandment, so worshiping God by representing the divine in any graphic way was considered idolatry. Other ancient civilizations imagined strange beasts as well, but they were capable of being represented in painting or sculpture easily, usually being a combination of human and animal features. The centaur had a man's torso and a horse's body; a satyr had a man's torso with a goat's hindquarters; Medusa looked like a woman except that her hair was composed of snakes; and so on.

But the beasts described in biblical apocalyptic literature are almost impossible to recreate in a drawing; I think that is because the original hearers did not attempt to draw anything at all. Thus, the images of Revelation, like those in Ezekiel and Daniel, were meant to be interpreted intellectually and emotionally, rather than representationally. Since much of modern abstract painting and sculpture tries to have the same emotional and intellectual effect rather than representational accuracy, perhaps we are poised in our day to have a new appreciation of these images.

However, as Christianity spread throughout the Roman world, most Christians had a pagan rather than a Jewish upbringing; they desired to visualize and represent the written descriptions of this book and all of Sacred Scripture. Furthermore, as the gospel spread throughout Western Europe, converts to Christianity tended to take whatever beliefs, mythology, and descriptions they had about the spiritual world and the occult and simply graft them onto the strange images in Revelation. Works such as the fourteenth-century tapestries from Angers, France, which are the illustrations for this study, are thus somewhat bizarre for sacred iconography. But they convey immense spiritual power and faith. So even as we appreciate that power, it is helpful to remember that the original visionary and hearers and readers of this book most probably did not try to draw a picture of what was described; they read it with their hearts and inscribed the imagery there alone.

In addition to the graphic arts, another important aspect of Greek and Roman culture that was not to be found in Jewish culture was the theater.

INTRODUCTION

But the formerly pagan descendants of the Greco-Roman culture continued the tradition of the theater as part of religious worship even as they became Christian. In the Middle Ages, churches were the place where liturgical dramas of mystery and morality plays were performed. It has been said that the book of Revelation would make a good play, with angels and beasts appearing on stage and acting out their conflicts while real trumpets sound their blasts and stage fire falls from the rafters. It undoubtedly has been the inspiration over the centuries for countless dramas about the fight between good and evil; but in the tradition of the Hebrew prophets, *this book says it is to be read and heeded, not performed.*

The Devil, Satan, and the Beasts

Finally, a problem with Revelation is that it makes many Christians today very uncomfortable to speak of the devil or to imagine evil personified as a powerful and real presence in the world. Although the Greek of the Lord's Prayer can just as correctly be translated, "deliver us from *the evil one*," it is too mythological and naïve an idea for many of us to conceive of an actual force of evil trying to corrupt and destroy the children of God. We certainly think it is absurd to think of a figure with horns and a tail, pitchfork in hand, who can suddenly make an appearance and then just as suddenly disappear in a cloud of sulphurous smoke. In Revelation, however, the forces of evil are personified and described in horrible detail.

It is clear in Revelation that only with the aid of the Lamb That Was Slain can we hope to endure and not go over to the dark side. Endurance here above all means not committing apostasy—that is the worst fate that could befall us, far worse than death. It is impossible to skip these parts of the book and move on to the beautiful scenes, as we sometimes do with some of the hard sayings of Jesus from the Gospels. The key ideas of this book, that suffering is an inevitable part of life, that forces of evil conspire to tempt and seduce the children of God, and that somehow suffering can be redemptive in God's economy, are not welcome in our worldview today. We want to eliminate all suffering, even if by so doing we remove all challenge and purification from our lives. The early Christians, on the other hand, prayed they would be able to withstand the trials that they *knew* would come; and story after story from Scripture and from early writings tells of Christians rejoicing that they had been found worthy to suffer for the sake of the gospel.

INTRODUCTION

The book of Revelation is describing those trials in the vivid language of Satan, the beasts, the harlot, pestilence, fire, and poison. Many Christians today in parts of Africa and Asia could describe their recent experiences in just those terms. There just does not seem to be an adequate explanation for the cruelty and slaughter human beings inflict upon each other without personifying evil as a force to be reckoned both within the human soul and without in the world at large. This book, written for people facing horrible persecution in their day, has brought courage and hope to people like them ever since. Even if we do not want to have the chance to suffer for our Lord, we can be strengthened by the faith and courage of those who have endured when our own trials come. For come they will, whether our feel-good psychology today prepares us for it or not. The teenage gunmen in schools, the crack addict waiting for us in the parking lot, and the bad news from the medical lab tests, as well as tornadoes, hurricanes, lightning, floods, droughts, traffic accidents, and now terrorist attacks that kill thousands of civilians in one morning are very much a part of life today. Are these not plagues and trials very like those seen in Revelation?

1

The Seer and the Vision

> The revelation of Jesus Christ, which God gave him to show to his servants what must soon take place; and he made it known by sending his angel to his servant John, who bore witness to the word of God and to the testimony of Jesus Christ, even to all that he saw. (Rev 1:1–2)

THIS IS THE FIRST verse of the last book; and it names the content of that book—a revelation *of* Jesus Christ *by* God *to* his servant John. The nouns, "revelation," "Jesus," "Christ," "God," "servant," and "John" are the basis of that content; it is the prepositions which show the crucial relationships between them.

The Greek word for "revelation" is *apocalypse*; that word does not mean something hidden and secret but just the opposite, something open and displayed for all who care to look and see. It is worth noting here that *apocalypse* originally did not have any necessary association with dreadful events and cataclysms. It was this particular book that introduced the notion that *apocalypse* is a synonym for horrible destruction, such as in the title of the film about the Vietnam war, *Apocalypse Now*. The fact that the message of the original Apocalypse, the Apocalypse to John, is one of ultimate hope and joy, of the vindication of the righteous and faithful, is often lost in our time.

God himself is the author of this revelation. The author presupposes that everyone knows and believes in God. Although he is living in a pagan world, and writing in the language of Homer and Aristotle to citizens and denizens of the Roman Empire, his audience is the tiny new "world" of Christians who know who the one and only God is. That one true God is the God of the Hebrew Scriptures which we now call the "Old Testament." It is He whom Jesus called "Father" in his earthly life and whom he taught his followers to address as "Our Father" in prayer. If God, then, has given his servant John a revelation, his testimony is not to be discounted or disbelieved.

What is the content of this revelation? It says it is a revelation of Jesus Christ. But the story of Jesus's earthly life and ministry, his miracles, teachings, suffering, death, and resurrection, are to be found in the four Gospels. There must be something new here, something not to be found in the Gospel accounts for this vision to be called a revelation of Jesus Christ and for it to be accorded this place of honor as the closing book of Holy Scripture. The tradition of the church is that this work is in fact the last written of all the books of the New Testament, so its place at the end is simply chronological order. But the more important point is that its place at the end is because of its subject matter: it is a vision of the end, not just the chronological end of this world but the *telos*, the end, or aim, of the life, death, and resurrection of Jesus the Christ.

The new revelation is that this end encompasses all of creation: that Christ will be all in all, just as Saint Paul had interpreted the prophecy of Isaiah, and that the Christ, understood as the sacrificial Passover Lamb who was slain to assure life for those who partake of it and trust in its blood, will be upon the throne of God. This last book of the Bible, then, is a vision of the risen Christ in glory, of Christ after the ascension recorded in Luke and Acts. It answers the question so many early Christians asked, "Where is Christ now?" by showing Christ in heaven, ascended and seated at the right hand of the Father, giving imagery to the words of the Nicene and Apostles' Creeds. In it he is seen in the light of eternity, revealed as the Savior of the world and ruling with the Father in heaven from whence he came.

This revelation, therefore, is about the fulfillment of the promise Jesus made to the repentant thief on the cross, "Truly I say to you, today you will be with me in Paradise," and his assurance to Thomas and the disciples, "In my Father's house are many rooms; . . . I go to prepare a place for you."[1] We might ask the question, "What is paradise like?" or say, "Tell me about the place you are preparing for us in your Father's house." In reply we have this revelation; all people who repent and turn to him, as did the disciples and

---

1. Luke 23:43; John 14:2.

the thief, can glimpse here the place promised to them by Jesus. A heavenly city is revealed where people from all tribes and nations gather at last in the mystical presence of Jesus before the throne of God for all eternity. God has revealed in this vision what we who cling to Christ in hope can expect—that is, what it means to be with Jesus in paradise.

Finally, it is important that it is a particular individual named John who claims to have received this revelation. He also tells us that he is a servant of God who has suffered for his faith by being banished to the island of Patmos in the Aegean Sea. The tradition of the church, as we discussed in the introduction, is that this John is the "beloved disciple" who wrote the Gospel of John and the Epistles of John. The tapestry depicting John on the Island of Patmos, the very first one of the series, has disappeared.

Whether or not we assume that the author of the book is the one whom the early church identified as "the disciple whom Jesus loved," who also wrote the Fourth Gospel and the letters, let us turn to the stated purpose of the revelation. It is to show to all the servants of God "what must soon take place." The highly symbolic language is supposed to be incomprehensible to unbelievers, as is greatly to be desired in times of persecution, and it relies heavily upon knowledge of the entire Old Testament as well as the teachings of Jesus on the part of its readers. But it does not impart an obscure, hidden message to a select few who have some special initiation and instruction other than baptism and faith in Jesus as Lord. Although people often think it is designed to encode a secret message, it is really designed to reveal a perfectly clear message to all *believers*. That is the source of its timelessness and universality. It does not, however, seek to explain the Christian faith to those outside, as does the book of Acts, for example, nor does it seek to evangelize by including sermons and teachings of Jesus or the apostles, as the other books of the New Testament do. In this respect the Revelation to John is like a church building with stained glass windows. From the outside the windows do not have much beauty, purpose, or meaning; but from the inside they are beautiful, instructive, and awe-inspiring for faithful people in their worship of Almighty God.

God sends his angel, or messenger, to John, who later writes down what he is shown as he is told to do. He calls it testimony from Jesus Christ. The Word of God which became flesh is now giving testimony to his servants so that everyone who hears it can "keep" what is written—remember it, in other words, and act upon that knowledge. "Servant" is an important word here: John is a servant of God who is delivering a message to the other servants of God. The concept of the servant of God is from the Old

Testament, especially from the second part of Isaiah, wherein the suffering that the servant of God would undergo for the sake of others is foretold. Jesus shows himself to be the fulfillment of the prophet's words by being the perfect servant of God, obedient unto death. Jesus teaches his disciples that the model for being his follower is service, saying, "I am among you as one who serves."[2] John is a faithful servant if he heeds the vision and writes it down for the benefit of the other servants of God as he is commanded to do: "Blessed is he who reads aloud the words of the prophecy, and blessed are those who hear, and who keep what is written therein; for the time is near."[3]

Not everyone receives a vision, but everyone can hear it and read it and keep it if it is proclaimed by the one to whom it is given. Keeping a vision means holding it close to heart, believing its promises, and abiding by its directives. Those who do will be blessed. Blessedness, of course, means enjoying the favor and eternal presence of God, dwelling in the house of the Lord forever, as the Twenty-Third Psalm puts it. Describing that dwelling place and that destiny is the content of the vision in the rest of the book.

There is a sense of urgency added at the end of this passage: "For the time is near." Although Jesus said that even the angels in heaven do not know the moment when God will bring in his kingdom, he tells John here that it is close at hand. Christians have never ceased trying to figure out a literal date for Christ's promised second coming, especially by using this book. But the temptation to decode God's promise in such a way is just succumbing to the ancient temptation of our first parents in the garden of Eden, the desire "to be like God, knowing good and evil."[4] It seems attractive; it is seductive; and it is a snare and a delusion. The righteous are to live by faith, as the prophet Habakkuk reminds us, not by esoteric knowledge which claims to know the mind of God. "Near" should be taken like "at hand," in the words of Jesus in the Gospels, as in his proclamation, "The kingdom of God is at hand."[5] God's kingdom is very near each moment, and at the same time it beckons to us as the eternal moment. Eternity must always be in the present moment; for the past stretches out behind us, and we can only remember it, whereas the future does not yet exist nor do we know how much of it will be our lot. The day of our death, be it sooner or later, full of years or cut off in our youth, is the only day which we know will come; so it is very near. On that day, for each

---

2. Luke 22:27.
3. Rev 1:3.
4. Gen 3:5.
5. Mark 1:15.

of us, the day of the Lord is at hand. The message is then for us in this time and for all servants of God in every time, for all times and days and years are equally near to God.

ANNOUNCING MESSAGES TO SEVEN CHURCHES

> John to the seven churches that are in Asia;
> Grace to you and peace from him who is and who was and who is to come, and from the seven spirits who are before his throne, and from Jesus Christ the faithful witness, the first-born of the dead, and the ruler of kings on earth. To him who loves us and has freed is from our sins by his blood and made us a kingdom, priests to his God and Father, to him be glory and dominion for ever and ever. Amen. Behold, he is coming with the clouds, and every eye will see him, every one who pierced him; and all the tribes of the earth will wail on account of him. Even so. Amen. (Rev 1:4–6)

Having thus introduced the significance and purpose of his book, John relates messages from Jesus to specific Christian churches in Asia, greeting them with "grace and peace" from "him who is and who was and who is to come, and from the seven spirits who are before his throne, and from Jesus Christ, the faithful witness, the first-born of the dead, and the ruler of kings on earth." This three-fold greeting is an early Trinitarian expression, for the first phrase refers to the Father, the seven spirits seem to refer to the Spirit of God working in and for each of the seven churches, and Jesus is the faithful witness. And each of his followers is being exhorted to become a faithful witness as well.

The universality of the vision is explicit: Jesus rules all the kings of the earth, when he comes with the clouds every eye will see him, and, when they do, *all* tribes will wail because those who pierced him are from all tribes, not just the leaders of his own people, the Jews, or the Romans who executed him or the actual people alive at the time and in the street who shouted, "Crucify him." That is all of us in every place and time whom he loves, for whom he shed his blood, whom he has made a kingdom of priests. While we were yet sinners Christ died for us, is the way Paul puts it. John's words evoke an image, a scene, as one would expect from someone recounting a vision, but the message is the same as Paul's. Who cannot but wail when we recognize him and realize what we did?

The words of the Lord God follow: "I am the Alpha and the Omega,"[6] the first and last letters of the Greek alphabet. Writing down the vision is what John has been commanded to do. We who read it are reading letters just as he who writes it is writing letters. Everything that can be written is the story of God, he seems to be saying, and the fact that we can symbolize thought and experience in the written word is a manifestation of the image of God in which we were formed. Notice that the title "Lord God" is from the Hebrew Scriptures, the Greek translation of the Hebrew one finds in the Septuagint, *Adonai Elohim*, which is itself a combination of titles for the Eternal One whose name is ineffable and unpronounceable. The title *adonai*, or "Lord," was substituted for the sacred Tetragrammaton, YHVH, whenever the text was read aloud; and in the Septuagint it was simply translated with the Greek word for "Lord," *kyrios*. The teaching implied in this usage is that God is our Lord and we are called to be his faithful servants just like Mary of Nazareth, who says to the angel Gabriel, "Behold, I am the *servant* of the Lord."[7]

> I John, your brother, who share with you in Jesus the tribulation and the kingdom and the patient endurance, was on the island called Patmos on account of the word of God and the testimony of

---

6. Rev 1:8.
7. Luke 1:38; emphasis added.

Jesus. I was in the Spirit on the Lord's Day, and I heard behind me a loud voice like a trumpet saying, "Write what you see in a book and send it to the seven churches, to Ephesus and to Smyrna and to Pergamum and to Thyatira and to Sardis and to Philadelphia and to Laodicea." (Rev 1:9–11)

John calls himself their brother because he shares with them the good and the bad that come with being a Christian—tribulation, the kingdom, and patient endurance when persecuted. He testifies that he was exiled for his faith on the island of Patmos, which may very well mean that he was called before the civil authorities to deny his faith and refused. There, as he was in the Spirit on the Lord's Day, he heard a voice telling him to write what he sees and send it to these churches. Hearing, seeing, and writing are all a part of the command. The Spirit is the origin of the vision; because he is in the Spirit, he can hear and see what the Father and the Son have to reveal to him. Here and in many places in this vision one can see the linking of the Father, the Son, and the Holy Spirit which the church will develop into the doctrine of the Trinity in the coming generations.

The Lord's Day means Sunday, the first day of the week, which became the day of worship for Christians because it was the day of the resurrection of Christ. His vision is therefore grounded in a certain day, a definite time which has specific religious significance. This vision is something that happened to him on a certain day of his life. But the day of the Lord is also the coming day—the day foretold by the Hebrew prophets and by Jesus of Nazareth. In a sense John is telling us that his vision *on* the Lord's Day is a vision *of* the Lord's Day—the eternal day that he will describe in the coming chapters.

Each church is an actual congregation of that day; but we must remember that the number seven connotes perfection, so these messages were also intended at the time to be taken to heart by all Christians who were to read this vision. Jesus commands John to write his words to the angels who guard each church, who then are to give the message to the faithful people of each church. Or, one could say, that when the church receives the written message from John, the angel guides them in interpreting and heeding it. Since they have been preserved as part of Sacred Scripture, these messages are still, through the power of the Holy Spirit and the communion of saints, addressed to every church anywhere and in any time. So, as you read them, think of your own parish and of yourself as a faithful member thereof. What applies to you?

The Last Word

The second tapestry depicts seven Gothic churches which look like the cathedrals of the fourteenth century, each with an angel perched on top of its pointed roof. Imagine the angel that is over your parish church: a guardian angel who receives the written message from Christ himself and is charged with delivering the message to the members. Such is the care that Christ has for his body on earth, the church, that "he has given his angels charge over them to keep them in all their ways," as it says in the Ninety-First Psalm.[8] What a comforting and yet sobering thought!

> Then I turned to see the voice that was speaking to me, and on turning I saw seven golden lampstands, and in the midst of the lampstands one like a son of man, clothed with a long robe and with a golden girdle round his breast; his head and his hair were white as white wool, white as snow; his eyes were like a flame of fire, his feet were like burnished bronze, refined as in a furnace, and his voice was like the sound of many waters; in his right hand he held seven stars, from his mouth issued a sharp two-edged sword, and his face was like the sun shining in full strength. (Rev 1:12–16)

This is the first description in the vision of the risen Christ. That it is couched in language and symbols from the vision in the book of the prophet Daniel shows us how important our prior religious experience and education is to enable us to articulate the inexpressible—the reality of an encounter with

8. Verse 11.

the divine. Once when the appearances of the virgin Mary to the children of Medjugorje were very much in the news, a Roman Catholic priest and I pondered why it is that a group of devout Baptists or other Protestants have never reported an appearance of the virgin Mary to them. We speculated that perhaps God sends His messengers to us in a way in which we are somehow prepared to receive their message. Otherwise, their appearance, like many a miracle, goes unnoticed.

The theme that recurs throughout all the theophanies of Scripture is just this: God comes in unexpected ways, to be sure, but always to each individual in a way that she has been uniquely prepared to comprehend—eventually. The three visitors receive Abraham and Sarah's hospitality offered according to the custom in that day; their divine provenance is revealed as they share the meal. Moses the shepherd sees a bush that is burning but not consumed; after he turns aside to inspect this strange sight, the voice of God Himself speaks. Isaiah the priest is in the temple when he sees a vision of the Lord in His heavenly temple, surrounded by the incense and hymns of the liturgy. Mary of Nazareth receives a visit from an angel with an amazing message; she knows the ancient story of barren Sarah who was past childbearing, "Is anything too hard for the Lord?"[9] so she responds in faith to the call to bear God's son while she is yet a virgin. When she goes to visit her kinswoman Elizabeth, who was, like Sarah, past menopause when she conceived, and the child within Elizabeth's womb leaps in greeting of the child within Mary's, the private feminine world of conception and gestation becomes a proclamation of salvation for the world. So it is that John receives a vision on the Lord's Day, a day of prayer and manifestations of the Spirit, and the words of the visionary prophets of his people, especially Daniel, Ezekiel, and Zechariah, give him the concepts and symbols with which to begin to recount his experience.

The voice like a trumpet prefigures both the actual trumpets which will sound later and voices of the heavenly choirs which will sing over and over in this vision. It is through hearing that John first is approached. When he turns to look at the speaker, he sees seven lampstands. In the book of the prophet Zechariah, lampstands are symbols for the temple; they here represent the seven churches because the body of Christ, the church, is the new temple, the one he said would be raised up in three days after it is destroyed. Then John sees one "like a son of man," a description from the vision of the prophet Daniel and the way Jesus referred to himself throughout

---

9. Gen 18:14.

the Gospel accounts. The "Son of Man" is the Messiah—the anointed one of God foretold by the prophets. Although Christians believe that the title "Son of God" means Jesus is the Messiah, it is actually the title "Son of Man" which carries that weight from the Hebrew Scriptures. "Son of God" emphasizes that Jesus is divine and the savior of the whole world.

Since Jews did not make graven images, as we have discussed in the introduction, their verbal imagery is primarily intellectual, not visual. One must think of the symbolism of all the elements in this description and the power of finding them revealed all together at once in one person. The description of this "Son of Man" is hard to imagine, much less draw or paint, but that did not deter the artist of Angers. In the third tapestry, this person is clothed with a long robe with a golden girdle, but his feet of burnished bronze are depicted very clearly. He has white hair like wool or snow, eyes like flames, and his face was shining like the sun in full strength. The face of this figure in the tapestry is indeed the focal point of the scene. In the tapestry the seven stars which he holds in his right hand appear very small in the palm of the hand extended to touch John's back as he does obeisance to him at his feet. The lampstands are single candelabra, arranged four to his right and three to his left. The number seven is a central unifying theme of the vision, and the many series of sevens are divided first four and then three, when they must be divided. It would be difficult to depict his voice like the sound of many waters, but the sharp two-edged sword issuing from his mouth cuts across the line of the candelabra with a dramatic sense of imbalance. The sharp two-edged sword in Heb 4:12 and Eph 6:17 is the gospel; but the sword also connotes the righteous judgment of the Lord which he speaks with his mouth.

John's reaction is fear, just as it always is for anyone confronted with an encounter with God. He falls down as if dead but is reassured in the very words Jesus spoke to his disciples when he approached them walking on the water, "Fear not." "I am the first and the last and the living one."[10] The first and the last is the Lord God who is Alpha and Omega, who was and is and is to come. Jesus is saying, obliquely, that he is one with the Father. He goes on to say that he died and now lives and has the keys to death and Hades, the greatest fears of mankind then and now, and he tells John to write what he sees. John obeys and writes so that the seven churches and the church universal, his brothers and sisters then and in generations yet to

---

10. Rev 1:17–18.

come, can calm our fears and realize that it is he, our Lord, who is speaking to us through the written words.

In this vision, first the seer sees something and describes it; the astute reader may know or guess the meaning of the symbolism. But, just as Jesus sometimes explains a parable to his disciples after he has told it, the angel then explains the meaning of the components of the vision to the apostle John to make it crystal clear. Both the explicit meaning, which carries a topical message, and the symbolic meaning, which is multivalent and resonant, are provided to the faithful. Symbols of course participate in the reality to which they point, so the power of the symbols in this book reverberate throughout the history of the church as each new generation enters into their meaning. Jesus explains that the seven candlesticks in the vision at the end of chapter 1 are these churches, and the seven stars which are in his right hand are their angels.

In the Bible, the number seven signifies perfection or completeness; it is the number of days in the week, a part of the original plan of creation. The seventh day, the day of rest, of worship, prefigures the eternal day of the Lord which is revealed in this vision. The seven lampstands, which stand for the seven churches, symbolize also all the churches there are and have been and will be. Each church is to be a lamp set on a stand, in the words of Jesus, not a light hidden under a bushel. Their purpose is to give light to the world. Each church has her own special angel watching over her, the stars in the Lord's right hand. What a precious promise to us who worship and work in our congregations—there is an angel watching over Mount Olivet in Algiers, Saint Peter's in Rome, Saint Paul's in London, "Saint Swithin's-in-the-Swamp," First Presbyterian in San Antonio, Highland Park Methodist in Dallas, and over L'Incarnation with its thatched roof and dirt floor in Haiti, as well as over the two or three that are gathered together without a building but in the Lord's name.

2

Revealing the Messages to Four Churches

IN THE SECOND CHAPTER of Revelation the messages of Jesus to the seven churches in Asia begin. The literary form of the first message is repeated in all the letters to the churches: first there is a highly symbolic epithet for Jesus who gives the message, then a recital of the good things the church has done followed by a recital of their shortcomings. Then follows a message of repentance, judgment, or warning about trials to come. Finally, there is the admonition to hear this message with the heart, not just the ears, and a promise of heavenly reward for those who do. The rewards promised should not be taken as a teaching that one's good works earn one's way into heaven. Rather, they are meant to engender a longing for the future into which God has called the faithful.

EPHESUS

The first message is to the church at Ephesus. They are known for their good works, labor, patience, and intolerance of evil, but also for false teachers in their midst. Although they have not fainted and grown tired in their labors, Jesus has something against them. Implying the image of the church as the bride and Christ as the bridegroom, an image which will figure prominently later in the vision, he says they have not the same love they had for him at first. They should remember from whence they have fallen and return to that first fervor, just as married couples sometimes need to be recalled to the first intense love which brought them together in the beginning. There is a warning as well as that somewhat wistful plea; if they do not return to their first fervor, Jesus will remove their candlestick from its place. (Imagine the second piece of the tapestry with one of the seven candlesticks missing from its place!) The warning would seem to be not so much a threat as a fact. As the early seventeenth century English poet John Donne wrote, "Love is a growing, or full constant light, / And his first minute, after noon, is night."[1]

They are commended for hating the deeds of the Nicolaitans. The necessity of discerning and choosing between competing loyalties was of supreme importance to those who were facing persecution and to whom false teachers were a threat to their very survival as Christians. In Hebrew idiom one either hates or loves, there is no middle ground; they must "hate" those who follow false prophets. The message concludes with the typical exhortation of the prophets, from the Old Testament to Jesus in the Gospels: "He that has an ear to hear, let him hear." Receiving the message requires attention on the part of the hearer—not just a passive reception in the strictly physical sense of hearing.

The promise for those who do hear and endure and overcome is that Jesus himself "will give [them] to eat of the tree of life, which is in the midst of the paradise of God."[2] The mention of the tree of life recalls the tree in the midst of the garden of Eden. To prevent the man and the woman who had tasted of the forbidden tree of the knowledge of good and evil from "reaching out their hand" and eating from it and living forever, God expelled them from the garden. Now Jesus promises to his followers that they will eat of it because that tree is now in another place, not Eden but paradise. It is important to realize that Jesus is not promising a return to Eden; there can be no going backwards in the Christian view of life (in distinction to a cyclical view, such as some other religions have). What we do is done once and for all and has eternal significance. But there is a future which is God's promise to us, and in that future, there is all that we have longed for, all that we have lost and lamented the loss of; and there is more than that, there is life itself, unmarred by our sin but still adorned with our praise and prayers, our good deeds, and our sacrifices.

---

1. Donne, "Lecture upon the Shadow," stanza 2.
2. Rev 2:7.

SMYRNA

The next message is to the angel of the church in Smyrna, from "the first and the last, which was dead, and is alive."³ The epithet for Jesus here refers to both his preexistence, and his *telos* as the end of all things in creation, and to his earthly life, which ended in death and resurrection. Jesus first tells them that he knows their works, their tribulations, and their poverty, but reminds them that they have true riches in heaven. Furthermore, he knows what they have been enduring from those who are of the synagogue of Satan. (How comforting to be assured in these words that Jesus knows what we sometimes endure in the internecine strife within our churches and communities!) His message to them is not to fear what they are about to suffer—trials which will include imprisonment and perhaps death. They are told to be faithful unto death, for then Jesus will give them a crown of life.

So the death and new life of Jesus, with which he begins his message, is to be their pattern. As Paul says, if we participate in Jesus's death, we can be assured we will also participate in his resurrection. Let him who has an ear to hear, hear; to the one who overcomes the terror of death and perhaps torture which lies in the path of these Smyrnans, Jesus says the Spirit promises that there will be no more terror, suffering, or death. No "second death" for them. Just as we sing in the Easter hymn about Jesus, "And the passion that he bore—sin and pain can vex no more,"⁴ it will be true for us as well if we die a faithful death. No matter how fearsome it may be, it can only happen once. The promise is given to overcome the dread of death with the hope of joy beyond.

PERGAMUM

The third message, to the angel of the church in Pergamum, is "the words of him who has the sharp two-edged sword."⁵ That is the sword of the gospel, according to Paul and to the author of Hebrews, and the sword is in the mouth of Jesus, the one "like the son of man" who is speaking. The gospel is good news and a call to repentance at the same time; like a two-edged sword, it cuts both ways. We cannot receive the grace without acknowledging our deep need for it. In the same pattern we have seen, Jesus first

---

3. Rev 2:8.
4. Alexander, "He Is Risen," stanza 2.
5. Rev 2:14.

commends them for their good works even in the place of Satan, and their holding fast even to the point of martyrdom for one of their number, Antipas. But he has a few things against them as well: they have allowed those who preach false doctrine to continue among them.

We think today of the necessity of tolerance for different ways of looking at even the Christian faith, and are uncomfortable with this message of intolerance for false doctrine. But we must try to understand the climate of persecution at the end of the first century when this was written. Christians were a small minority in a culture that thought they were dangerous and/or deluded. The danger of diluting or corrupting a new faith that still was largely oral in its transmission was a real threat to the existence of the church, as were self-appointed teachers of philosophy who tried to persuade communities to adopt one of the other, more fashionable doctrines current at the time. There were no libraries full of Scriptural commentaries and theological discourses on Christian doctrine for confused peopled to consult when false teaching arose. So false teachers were dangerous indeed.

Jesus calls upon the faithful in Pergamum to repent, or else. If they do not, he will come quickly to fight against them with the sword in his mouth. (Remember this message when we get to the last petition of this book, "Come, Lord Jesus" (Rev 22:20). The coming of Christ is what the church prays for every time we pray the prayer Jesus taught us. How often, however, do we remember that his coming is judgment as well as reward?) To those that hear and heed, and therefore overcome, Jesus will give them manna to eat. It is hidden manna that no one else can see, the food which comes from God, recalling Jesus's rebuke to Satan in the wilderness, "Man does not live by bread alone but by every word that proceeds from the mouth of God."[6]

There is another gift promised as well, a white stone on which the name of the one who receives it is written, a name that no one else in all the world will know—a secret, hidden name. That secret name is presumably the one written in the Book of Life, which comes into the vision soon. The intimacy between Jesus and each believer is thus emphasized with the giving of a new name, the sign in the Bible of a new relationship with God, and a secret name, like that between lovers or special friends. Notice also how the first temptation of Christ is recalled here—manna to eat, like that given to the Hebrews in the wilderness, and stones, not to be turned to bread and eaten but to be inscribed with our secret name. God gives us both out of love.

6. Matt 4:4.

THYATIRA

The fourth message is to the church at Thyatira, from the Son of God who has eyes like a flame of fire and whose feet are like burnished bronze. Notice how exactly the artist includes each detail of these descriptions in the tapestry, especially the reddened feet in contrast with the seer's white hands so close to them. No feet of clay here—we will not be disappointed when we see our Lord face-to-face, from head to toe. The Christians of Thyatira are commended for their faith and works and their patient endurance; but they are condemned for their tolerance! They have been tolerating a woman who calls herself a prophetess but who is really a Jezebel, beguiling and teaching them to follow idols, just as Jezebel, the wife of King Ahab, did to the Israelites in the days of the great prophet Elijah, who opposed her. There is no problem with having a woman in a position of leadership as prophetess; the problem is with this particular woman who practices immorality and induces them to eat food sacrificed to idols, a highly symbolic prohibition for gentile Christians we see commanded in the book of Acts and discussed again by Saint Paul in Corinthians.

Taking up the theme of infidelity to God as adultery in the manner of the Old Testament prophets, John warns that she will be thrown on a sickbed and that all who consort with her will suffer, and all her children will be stricken unless she repents. Like a true prophet, he offers her God's promise of forgiveness if she will only repent of her wickedness. An emphasis on works is part of this message—"I will give to each of you as your works deserve."[7] And they are urged to hold fast to what they have until Jesus comes. Then he will give to them "the morning star"—an epithet for himself symbolic of the new eternal day that is dawning.

---

7. Rev 2:23.

3

Revealing the Messages to Three More Churches

SARDIS

To the angel of the church in Sardis the seer is to write, "The words of him who has the seven spirits of God and the seven stars,"[1] that is, one who has the same attributes as God himself in the first greeting in Rev 1:5. Their reputation is great, but the Lord, who knows all hearts, knows otherwise. "You have the name of being alive, and you are dead."[2] This message is always apt for many churches in every age. It is so easy to rest on the laurels gained from a fine endowment or the former pastor's zeal and forget that a church, like a person, needs to grow in faith and works or it begins to die.

Jesus tells them to wake up and strengthen what remains, for it is on the point of death. There is a point beyond which rejuvenation is impossible, and they are almost there. His judgment seems harsh and his standard too high, for he says, "I have not found your works perfect in the sight of my God."[3] This recalls the words of Jesus in Matthew's Gospel: "Be ye perfect, as your Father in heaven is perfect."[4] It means, however, not that we are given

1. Rev 3:1.
2. Rev 3:1.
3. Rev 3:2.
4. Matt 5:48 KJV.

an impossible task and expectation to live up to, but rather that the standard by which we are to be judged is not of our own devising but of God's. Jesus goes on to say that if they will not repent and return to practicing what they have received and heard, he will come. But his coming will be like that of a dreaded thief in the night, not a cause of rejoicing. The theme of "Come, Lord Jesus," which encircles this whole book, is like the two-edged sword pictured in his mouth. His coming is deliverance and judgment.

Yet there are a few, a "righteous remnant," to use the Old Testament imagery, who have not soiled their garments; they will walk with Jesus and will also receive a white garment, for they are worthy. The African American spiritual, "Do Lord, Remember Me," expresses the confidence of those who believe that they will be among these few: "You wear the long white robe and I'll wear the crown." Jesus says he will not blot out their names from the Book of Life but rather will confess their names to God the Father and the angels. This message ends like the others with the words of the prophet Isaiah, which Jesus used often in his earthly ministry, "He who has ears to hear, let him hear." Their resonance is that each of us is free to hear the message or not to listen. If even a great sinner truly hears, he or she can decide to heed the message and be saved.

PHILADELPHIA

The epithet Jesus chooses for himself in the next message for the Philadelphians is "the holy one, the true one, who has the key of David, who opens and no one shall shut, who shuts and no one opens."[5] The message continues this theme. He knows their works and has set before them an open door which no one is able to shut—for they have been faithful, not denying his name and patiently enduring persecution. Those who oppose them are called the synagogue of Satan, and they will have to come and bow down before these faithful people and learn who it is that God has loved. So having one's enemies see one's vindication, as in the Twenty-Third Psalm, "Thou settest a table for me in the presence on mine enemies,"[6] is a confirmation of God's love, a confirmation for which we all long when we are being oppressed in this earthly life. They also are urged to hold fast to what they have "so that no one may seize your crown,"[7] almost as if someone is

---

5. Rev 3:7.
6. Ps 23:5 KJV.
7. Rev 3:11.

trying to grab the crown off their heads. Always there is the sense of a fight going on, spiritual warfare in which those who are vigilant, determined, and faithful will emerge victorious.

The writer must deliver the message to cheer them on and assure them that their sufferings are precious in the sight of God, who is watching every moment of the struggle. Those who conquer will be made into pillars of the temple of God, as we still say of someone who is a staunch Christian, "She is a pillar of the church." We will be part of God's temple, holding it up. And again, there is the writing of names: each faithful person will have the name of God inscribed on her or him, along with the name of the city of God, and Jesus's "own new name." The message ends with the refrain, "He who has ears to hear," like the one before it.

LAODICEA

The final message is perhaps the most famous, and the most frightening; it is the words to the church at Laodicea. These words are from "the Amen, the faithful and true witness, the beginning of God's creation,"[8] from the last word (Amen) to the beginning, in which the word acted by creating the world. And it is a word of judgment:

> I know your works: you are neither hot nor cold. Would that you were hot or cold! So, because you are . . . neither cold nor hot, I will spew you out of my mouth. (Rev 3:15–16)

They think they are doing fine, so they do not acknowledge their need for God.

This message rings out through the ages to the church when it is no longer persecuted or in the minority but comfortable within the culture, filled with women and men of civic distinction, influence, and means. They think they are rich, but they are really "wretched, pitiable, poor, blind and naked."[9] They have not, in other words, used their ears to hear the true message of salvation. But there is hope for even them, if they will take the advice offered them. The theme of buying and selling, which will be prominent throughout this vision, is introduced here. These supposedly rich and happy people are advised to buy gold refined by fire so they may have true riches, white garments to clothe their spiritual nakedness, and

---

8. Rev 3:14.
9. Rev 3:17.

salve to anoint their eyes so that they at last can see. They are reminded that God reproves us because he loves us and wants us to repent and know the truth. The prophet's task is actually one of love; judgment is a supreme act of God's love, for without it we cannot learn, and turn, and be saved.

The conclusion of this message is also one of the most famous passages of Scripture and indeed is one of the most important assurances of Jesus to all of us—but most people do not realize that it is not from the Gospels but from the mouth of the risen and ascended Christ in Revelation: "Behold I stand at the door and knock; if any one hears my voice and opens the door, I will come in to him and eat with him, and he with me."[10] Holman Hunt's paintings, *The Light of the World*, one of which is in Keble College Chapel, Oxford, and one of which is in Saint Paul's Cathedral, London,[11] depict Christ with a lantern in his hand knocking at the door of a house which has no outside handle or doorknob. He promises to come in and eat with us as he did with the travelers to Emmaus on Easter evening, and then our eyes will be opened as theirs were. But each of us has to open the door. In the paintings, the implication seems to be that after we receive him, we are then to go out into the world with Him who has the light, not stay afraid or isolated within our own room; but the text in Revelation here does not mention a light. That is the artist's inspired addition.

The message concludes with the promise that he who conquers will sit with Christ on his throne, as he conquered and sat down on the throne with God the Father. Somehow, heaven in this vision is perfect bliss and satisfaction for all, sans hierarchy. This is a further understanding of what is meant by being "with me in paradise"—it means being "with me on the throne!" This promise gives concreteness to Saint Paul's words about the "weight of glory" and "the unsearchable riches of Christ," which are promised to the faithful.[12] We are moved to say, "Oh no, not me, I am not worthy." But it is the Lamb who is worthy enough for all of us, so we can either accept his invitation or decline it. In this promise we see the biblical origin of the Eastern Orthodox doctrine of *theosis*, or becoming divine, as the ultimate destiny of those who have united themselves to Christ. The one who has ears, let him or her hear what the Spirit has to say to the churches—then and now and forevermore.

---

10. Rev 3:20.
11. There are two original but nearly identical paintings with this title by Hunt.
12. 2 Cor 4:17; Eph 3:8.

4

Visions of God in Heaven

NOW THAT THE INTRODUCTORY messages to the seven churches have been given, the first of seven series of seven visions each begins. These visions reveal what must soon happen in heaven and on earth. The purpose of the visions is to warn and encourage all Christians everywhere by assuring them that God is in charge, the Lamb is upon the throne, and God will win in the end. The trials and tribulations that befall the saints on earth are signs of how close that end is. All faithful people must be steadfast and realize that no matter how bad things seem to get, the meaning behind these events is that God is bringing in His kingdom very soon. The first three visions are of the glory of God, the risen and ascended Christ, and the heavenly host of elders, angels, and martyrs assuring us, in the words of Robert Browning, "God's in His Heaven / All's right with the world,"[1] or perhaps we should say, "All will be right with the world—soon!"

John looks and sees in heaven an open door; a voice like a trumpet says, "Come up hither, and I will show you what must take place after this."[2] It is the end of all history, revealed in heaven in the presence of God. At once he is "in the Spirit," and the vision begins. The fourth tableau of the first section of the tapestries depicts what the seer sees: one seated upon the throne, surrounded by twenty-four thrones with elders seated on them, a rainbow like an emerald around the throne, flashes of lightning, torches of fire, and a sea of glass in front of him. This description of God is confusing to depict literally—how can a person look like jasper and carnelian? But the fourth tapestry has the colors of red and green around the figure on the throne and has the rainbow, as two rainbows meeting as two arches, or bows, joined. Remember the symbolism of the rainbow in Genesis: it is a sign of peace because God takes his bow—an instrument of war—and places it in the clouds to remind sinful man that He will not destroy the earth by water again, and that forevermore the sun will follow the rain and seedtime follow harvest.

The twenty-four elders which John sees are shown in each of the four corners of the piece seated on their thrones in their white garments with their crowns upon their heads. The crystal sea surrounds the throne, and the seven lamps of the Spirit are behind it; and the book with its seals, the focus of the next chapter, is in the hands of the figure upon the throne. This figure, a representation of God the Father, nevertheless looks like the later figures in the tapestry of Jesus Christ in glory. John sees four living creatures like the ones in Ezekiel guarding the throne. They are full of eyes and, like the seraphim in Isaiah's vision, have six wings each and sing continually, "Holy, Holy, Holy, is the Lord God Almighty, who was and is and is to come."[3] These four creatures have long been identified in Christian iconography with the four evangelists: the angelic man for Matthew, the lion for Mark, the ox for Luke, and the eagle for John.

1. Browning, *Pippa Passes*, stanza 1.
2. Rev 4:1.
3. Rev 4:8.

The fifth tapestry depicts the conclusion of this vision—the ineffable joy of worship in heaven. Whenever the four creatures give glory and honor and thanks to Him who is seated on the throne, the twenty-four elders fall down and worship God also, casting their crowns before him and singing,

> Worthy art thou, our Lord and God,
> to receive glory and honor and power,
> for thou didst create all things,
> and by thy will they existed and were created.
> (Rev 4:11)

When we are face-to-face with God, the natural response is worship and praise. The way to express our deepest praise is in song. And in the presence of God, all other crowns are rightly offered to him in worship. The elders in the tapestry are in the process of casting them down: four are in the act of reaching for their crowns, while others have theirs in their hands, and still others are in the act of offering them. Two crowns are already in the foreground at God's feet. In the beloved hymn, "Holy, Holy, Holy," this scene is set to music, "All the saints adore thee, / casting down their golden crowns around the glassy sea."[4]

4. Heber, "Holy, Holy, Holy," stanza 2.

5

Who Is Worthy to Open the Book?

JOHN NOW SEES THAT there is a book in the right hand of the One that is seated upon the throne; it is sealed with seven seals. A "strong angel" asks the question, "Who is worthy to open the book and to break its seals?"[1] This is the Book of Life wherein the names of the faithful have been recorded. Somehow, opening the Book of Life is the key to getting the future started, as if all history has been awaiting the opening of this book. Only then can "what must take place after this"[2] begin to happen. John weeps because there is no one worthy to open it. In tapestry six we see John, here the central figure instead of being on the side as is usual, holding his head in tears. The angel on his right holding a scroll has gorgeous red and gold wings above and behind his head. The elder on his left is comforting John, taking his hand to point out there is one who is worthy to open it: the Lion of the tribe of Judah. But before we get to that passage, let us consider the question posed by the angel, "Who is worthy to open the book?"

The first question which comes to mind in response is, "Why doesn't God open the book himself?" The fact that God does not choose to open the book Himself implies that He wants there to be another person who is worthy to open his book and is sure that someone will eventually appear to do so. That is the desire of love—the desire for there to be another worthy to share in that love. The prior questions which then come to mind set our thoughts to the riddle of creation—why did God create the world at all, and why did God create man in his own image? The answer of the Bible is that God created the world out of love and created us in His image so there would be creatures able to freely love Him in return. The Bible tells of how the first man and woman turned away from God and followed their own desires instead of His commandments, and it chronicles how human beings have ever since chosen to defy God's will, even though God gave them the Law and the Prophets to show them the way.

Another observation which follows from these questions is that God evidently waits for us to do what we are able to do on our own; He does not intervene miraculously to solve all our problems. For example, as Canon John Fenton of Christ Church, Oxford, put it, God waited for human beings to discover that it was mosquitoes that caused malaria and yellow fever. Intrepid doctors and volunteers finally made that discovery in the early twentieth century and began to conquer those diseases, but God did not write that down in Scripture for us to know by revelation or reveal it to a prophet in a dream. The idea is that God wants human beings to use their minds and hearts and wills to exercise their dominion over the rest

---

1. Rev 5:2.
2. Rev 4:1.

of creation and patiently waits for us to accomplish on our own what we are capable of doing, much as a parent allows a child to make mistakes and learn at his own pace. Similarly in the moral realm, God waits until there is a human being righteous enough to open the Book of Life. He is not going to open it Himself because He knows that someday there will be the right person who will be able to do so.

For all of human history there has been no one worthy to open this book, the book of God's purpose for the world, until now. At last, with the life and death of Jesus, the One who was obedient unto death and whom God raised from the dead, there is one who is worthy to open the book. The elder, pointing him out to John, calls him by these epithets from the Old Testament: the Lion of Judah and the Root of David, who has conquered. They are names of triumph and strength, emphasizing his ancestor, the great King David, and his victory over death, through death, in fulfillment of the Law and the Prophets. It is only because of his worth that the names inscribed in this book can be read aloud in God's holy presence; in other words, it is only because of Jesus's merit that any other human being can hope to have his or her name written in God's Book of Life.

But when the worthy one is shown to John, he sees a not a lion or a king but a Lamb that has been slain, as is depicted in tapestry seven; for in this vision the high place of Christ in the glories of Heaven is always inseparable from the fact of his suffering and death. In the tapestry the Lamb is seen inside a medallion with the four creatures, the four evangelists who have told his story to the world, surrounding him. The Lamb here has his head bowed, as a sacrificial victim, reminiscent of Isaiah's suffering servant, who like a lamb was led to the slaughter. This is Jesus as the "Lamb of God who takes away the sins of the world," as John the Baptist called him in the Gospel of John.[3] The Lamb, although he has the banner of victory in his right foreleg, is bleeding from his feet and side to show the wounds of Jesus's crucifixion, and his halo carries a cross. John is back in his usual place on the side, as an observer instead of a participant; the twenty-four elders look on in amazement and sorrow. The seven eyes and seven horns which John sees, symbols of the Spirit of God, are left out of the picture here, leaving the simplicity and clarity of the portrait of the Lamb and his blood.

---

3. John 1:29.

The Lamb then takes the book from the right hand of God, and immediately the four beasts and elders begin to sing of how and why he is worthy to do so: "For thou wast slain and by thy blood didst ransom men for God from every tribe and tongue and people and nation."[4] The paradox of victory through suffering and death, of ransoming sinners by the sacrifice of the sinless one, is the theme of this song. Myriads of angels join in, "Worthy is the Lamb who was slain."[5] And then every creature in heaven and on earth, under the earth, or in the sea also praise the Lamb along with God: "To him who sits upon the throne and to the Lamb be blessing and honor and glory and might for ever and ever."[6] Jesus, the Lamb of God, is proclaimed worthy not only to open the book but to receive glory and worship with God, as God, as the four living creatures pronounce the "Amen" and the elders fall down in worship.

4. Rev 5:9.
5. Rev 5:12.
6. Rev 5:13.

6

Opening the Seals

IN ANOTHER SERIES OF sevens, there are seven seals guarding this book. The opening of the seals is also divided into a set of four and then three. As the Lamb opens each of the first four in turn, one of the four living creatures calls, "Come and see." Then, one by one, the famous "four horsemen of the Apocalypse" ride forth, and John is told to report faithfully what he sees. These horsemen are widely regarded as symbols of terror and destruction before the day of the Lord at the end of time. The first horseman, however, who comes forth on a white horse and receives a crown of power, is more coherently interpreted as a symbol of the reign of Christ, if not as Christ himself. His purpose is to stir up hope in the faithful that it is Christ who will ultimately conquer and reign, no matter how powerless his followers feel during their time of persecution. Even in the Roman Empire when all earthly power was concentrated in the hands of the supreme ruler, always named Caesar, and his legions, Christ has already gone forth to conquer. In tapestry eight we see the dignity of this rider and his white steed; he is poised like a noble knight in a tale of chivalry, the horse's forelocks echoing the rider's flowing beard. The bow in his hand recalls the bow which God placed in the clouds to remind Noah of His promise never again to destroy all living creatures with water. This bow, like the rainbow surrounding God upon his throne, is not only an instrument of warfare and victory but also a symbol of hope and trust in God's promises.

So, it is only after the promise that Christ will eventually triumph and that God's promises are to be trusted even in the most grievous adversity that the three dire horsemen are called forth. They represent the calamities unleashed on those who trust in the powers of this world, the wicked and faithful alike. After the opening of the second seal, when the second living creature by the throne of God calls out, "Come and see!" a man on a red horse the color of blood rides forth. He is given a sword and the power to take peace from the earth that men might kill one another, so he represents warfare. This panel of the tapestry has been lost.

After the third seal is broken open, the third creature calls out the same command, and the third horseman, on a black horse and carrying a balance in his hand, appears. The depiction of this horse and rider in the tapestry is obviously different from the noble form of the first horseman—he wears a red robe and looks backward as if unsure of himself. There is a snake in the grass in front of the horse's feet, an ominous appearance of that ancient serpent, Satan, loose in the world. There is a bird, however, in the tree above it, just as there is in the tapestry of the first horseman—a symbol of hope, perhaps, recalling the raven and the dove that Noah sent forth from the ark. The balance symbolizes famine; for when the price for wheat and barley becomes exorbitant, they must be weighed very carefully. A voice in the midst of the four creatures makes this clear, calling out the prices but saying that oil and wine are not to be touched—a strange reference to the luxuries of life. Again, the message is that the faithful should not despair even in the famine which warfare usually brings, for it is God who has sent these horsemen forth. The four creatures appear in the top left of the tapestry with their message on a scroll hanging down from a cloud. As we have seen, they symbolize the testimony of the four Gospels that assures us that these signs of the end, painful though they may be, are tokens of God's coming reign of justice and peace.

As the fourth seal is opened by the Lamb, the fourth creature says, "Come and See." The text does not say which beast is speaking; but since the beast in this tapestry is the eagle, representing Saint John, the artist must have imagined that the other beasts went in order of the Gospels, from Matthew the man, to Mark the lion, to Luke the ox, and so now it is John the eagle who speaks. This last horse is pale, or livid, and his horseman is death itself, represented in the tapestry as a skeleton. The text says that Hell or Hades follows him, perhaps upon the same horse; but the tapestry depicts Hell as a small temple protruding from the earth, giving a glimpse of the bowels of the earth wherein the damned reside in eternal flames, guarded by devils who push them back down. The blood red background of the panel symbolizes the flames of Hell and contrasts with the pale, bloodless color of the horse and the fleshless rider with the sword of killing in his hand. This fourth horseman is given power over a fourth of the earth, to kill with sword, famine, pestilence, and by means of earth's wild beasts. His mission sums up those of the two just before him—death and destruction—but one must remember that the first horseman, the emissary of Christ himself, assures us of God's final victory.

The use of fractions here and several other times when describing the amount of destruction which is to be allowed reminds us that God always saves a remnant of his creation. In the great flood, for example, Noah and his family and the male and female of each kind of animal in the ark are saved. But an interesting point about dealing with fractions is that one gets into an infinite regress. If one speaks of walking half the distance to a door, and then half of the remainder, and then half of the remainder, one will theoretically never get to the door, for there will always be a half portion of the original distance left to be traversed, however infinitesimally small. So it is significant that the destruction that God commands in these trials before the end is always to be of *only* a fraction of the creation—never is it a complete annihilation.

Now that the first group of four is complete, the fifth seal brings a different scene to John's eyes. For under the altar in Heaven, he now sees for the first time the souls of those who have already been slain for the word of God, those whose names are written in the book that is so soon to be opened. It is as if the progress of Heaven itself has been awaiting the coming of the one worthy to open those seals and set the future in motion. Their plea is for vengeance, not that God would forgive those who were killing them, as Jesus prayed on the cross and as Stephen did as he was being stoned. The fact that their desire is not commendable from a Christian point of view shows that they are still awaiting consummation as the blessed, even as their souls are protected in the holy place. It seems they still have a human point of view, even as they trust in God's final purpose. Their longing is for God to vindicate their deaths by showing His might; they wonder how long it must be before all the world will see the truth for which they suffered and died.

The desire for God to take vengeance on the enemies of the righteous, and to repay those who have tortured and slain them, moreover, is a frequent theme of the Psalms, those wonderful honest prayers of faithful people to their God. In the translation of the Book of Common Prayer, Psalm 94 begins,

> O Lord God of vengeance,
> O God of vengeance, show yourself.
> Rise up, O Judge of the world;
> give the arrogant their just deserts.
> How long shall the wicked, O Lord,
> how long shall the wicked triumph?

Now the souls of the faithful are still singing that old song, even under the altar in heaven. And God hears their prayers and answers them in His wisdom as is best for them. He gives them each a white robe, symbolizing the righteousness of Jesus in whom they have placed their confidence (these are the robes which will later be described as being washed in the blood of the Lamb), and they are told to rest a while longer until their number is complete. There is a sense of fatalism here—that there is a specific number of martyrs which will be finally enough to signal God to act decisively to end history. But it also can be seen as a directive to place one's faith in God, even after death, because one cannot know His infinite purpose. The saints in this thirteenth tapestry are depicted as all white, like ghosts to our modern imagination, and they vividly contrast with the blood-red platform upon which the altar rests, a reminder of the blood they have shed and of the blood of Christ. The chalice on the altar symbolizes the sacrifice of the blood of Christ and the sacrifice of their lifeblood, which is united to his.

They all look to God in entreaty and gratitude as His angel gives them their robes. God still provides for our needs, even after death; and it is significant that it is symbolized as clothing. Remember that the Lord gave animal skins to Adam and Eve as He expelled them from the garden of Eden, realizing their need for clothing more substantial and concealing than fig leaves. Clothing then, in the Bible, is a symbol of the necessity of human existence after the fall, and of God's providential care for his fallen creation. It is interesting that even in the world to come, we shall still be grateful for the garments which He will provide for us out of love.

From this passage also comes the common Christian practice of burying the faithful dead under the altar of the church. If that is where the souls of the faithful departed await the coming of the Kingdom in the last book of the Bible, then here on earth it is the most fitting place possible for the repose of one's earthly remains. A visitor to Saint Peter's in Rome, for example, may be surprised to see a skeleton lying in a glass coffin glass beneath a side altar near to the main entrance, but relics of saints are traditionally encased within altars of Roman Catholic and Anglican churches, we just do not see them very often. The altar of Saint Peter's is supposed to be over the grave of Saint Peter himself, as one can find out on the "Excavi" tour. And if there was no more room under the altar itself, the remains of the departed were placed in the floor and walls of the church and then outside in the churchyard, but still in hallowed ground. Still today, the cremated remains of a faithful person are often placed under the altar in the sanctuary if there must be a delay in placing them in a columbarium or grave. Indeed, since churchyards are scarce these days or the land needs to be used otherwise than as a graveyard, a church may build a wall of niches, or columbarium, on the church property to provide a final resting place for the ashes of the faithful close by the altar.

The saints whose remains are literally under the altar, or within the grounds of the church building, remind us of all the saints waiting in Heaven for the final consummation of God's will, and they are vividly recalled as part of "the company" in our imagination as we say, "Therefore with angels and archangels and with all the company of Heaven, we laud and magnify thy holy name, evermore praising thee and saying, 'Holy, Holy, Holy Lord God of Hosts, Heaven and Earth are full of thy Glory.'" And as in the familiar hymn, "The Church's One Foundation," the cry of the saints resonates through the centuries; as we identify with their longing and desire for vindication, we can share in their faith that there will be a consummation in God's good time:

> Yet saints their watch are keeping
> Their cry goes up, "How long?"
> And soon the night of weeping
> Shall be the morn of song.[1]

When the sixth seal is opened, the creation itself begins to come undone: the earth quakes, the sun darkens, the moon turns to blood and stars fall out of the sky, the fig tree sheds it fruit, the sky vanishes like a rolled-up scroll, and mountains and islands are moved. These natural catastrophes are similar to those predicted in the writings of Isaiah, and the theme emerges yet again that the God who created the cosmos and set the heavenly bodies and natural processes in motion can also bring chaos back. The rich and powerful, the kings and generals, along with all humanity, slave and free, hide in terror as they recognize that these calamities are the wrath of God, the One seated on the throne, and of the Lamb. The day of the Lord, which the Hebrew prophets and Jesus himself foretold, has arrived, and it is a day of wrath. They ask, "Who can stand before it" echoing Malachi's words, "But who may abide the day of his coming?"[2] This tapestry is lost, and with it ends the first set.

1. Stone, "Church's One Foundation," stanza 3.
2. Mal 3:2 KJV.

7

The Interlude Before the Seventh Seal

The first six seals have been opened quickly; but since opening the last seal will bring about the end, there is a pause before it is opened, both to emphasize its importance and to increase the sense of drama and foreboding and longing mixed together. It has been suggested that this work is like a melodrama, with an inevitable plot which seems to dash to its climax again and again, only to be diverted at the last moment in order for another facet of the story to be introduced. We do not know if the Revelation to John was meant to ever be read aloud from beginning to end; but if it were, it would be a thrilling story, always catching the listener just when one would think the end really has come, to reveal that there is more to see and more which must take place before the ultimate end. As a literary device, this method conveys the urgency of the message alongside the reality that one really does not know the day or the hour when God will bring in His kingdom. But the underlying and urgent theme is that this vision will be fulfilled, so all who believe that should be prepared and not despair in the meanwhile.

Before the seventh seal is opened and the future which must be actually arrives, four angels appear at the four corners of the earth, holding back the four winds. (There is only a fragment of this tapestry.) The way ancient mythology conceived of the earth was in sets of fours—four corners, four winds, four directions, etc.—and thus the number four is the number of earth. Three is the number of Heaven in Hebrew thought; for example, it is three angels who appear to Abraham and Sarah and who turn out to be the Lord God Himself. Since seven is the sum of the number of heaven and the number of earth, it is the perfect number. The four winds that the angels are holding back here represent the fury of God's righteous anger at the wickedness of the earth.

Another angel, who has the seal of God, ascends from the rising of the sun and calls with a loud voice to those four angels. This time the seal signifies the signature of God, the authenticity of this command, rather than a seal to close up the scroll and keep its contents secret. The command is to wait to release the winds that will harm the earth and sea and trees until the servants of God here on earth have been sealed upon their foreheads. We now have a third nuance of meaning for "seal," for this seal on their foreheads is to be a mark which will save them in the coming disaster, just as the blood of the Passover lamb wiped upon the lintels of their homes saved the Hebrews from the angel of death, the last plague of the exodus. It also recalls the lover's plea in the Song of Songs, "Set me as a seal upon your heart, as a seal upon your arm; for love is strong as death."[1] For out of love for us, Christ our Passover was sacrificed for us; out of love he seals those who love him so that, come what may, they will be marked as his own forever. We recall this passage in the rite of baptism when we make the sign of the cross on the forehead of the newly baptized and say the words, "You are sealed by the Holy Spirit in baptism and marked as Christ's own forever."

John now hears the number of those who are sealed read aloud: 144,000, twelve thousand out of each of the tribes of Israel. The American camp meeting spiritual "When the Roll Is Called Up Yonder I'll Be There" derives from this passage, bringing to mind as it does the innumerable roll calls of our lives when we must step forth and be counted and call out, "Here!" This is the last and most important time to be there!

---

1. Song 8:6.

THE INTERLUDE BEFORE THE SEVENTH SEAL

Then John sees the multitude of those who are to be sealed and saved, a great multitude from every nation and tribe and people. It is not just for the chosen people, the Jews, that our Lord died, but for all people everywhere who turn to him in faith. So, in contrast to the numbering of Israel, this vast array of people is so large that no human being can count them. God, however, has sealed each one and knows each one by name. They are clothed in white robes and wave palm branches and cry out, "Salvation belongs to our God who sits upon the throne and to the Lamb."[2] The angels, elders, and heavenly creatures join in their praise and fall on their faces before the throne saying, "Blessing and glory and wisdom and thanksgiving and honor and power and might be to our God forever and ever! Amen."[3] So again John hears the words of a hymn of praise and writes it down for the church to be able to join in the songs of heaven through the ages. In this tapestry this great multitude is depicted as an orderly file on the bottom row, with the elders above them and the angels above them; the four creatures surround the throne where God sits, in aspect like the depiction of the human Jesus but with the Lamb of God under His right arm like a pet and with the Book of Life open in His left hand.

2. Rev 7:10.
3. Rev 7:12.

The framework for explaining these visions is the question-and-answer pattern like that in Ezekiel's visions in the Old Testament. An elder here asks John who all these people are, to which he replies, "Sir, you know."[4] As always, John does not presume to interpret what he sees but waits for it to be explained to him by the heavenly guide. That means that we who read his account can trust his explanation, for it is of God and not of men. John learns from the angel here that these are those who have come out of the great tribulation—there will be a terrible disaster, but all this great multitude will come through it into heaven. And their white robes? They have been washed in the blood of the Lamb. The paradox of blood turning a robe white is again an intellectual image, not a literal one, and it recalls and develops the promise given by the Lord to the prophet Isaiah: "Though your sins be as scarlet, they shall be white as snow."[5] Actually, the artist gives the people in the tapestry all colors of robes to represent all humanity realistically; one can see the clothing of nobles, merchants, bishops, and kings.

The blessings that the elect will enjoy in heaven are enumerated in the poetic passage that follows. They will serve God day and night in his temple, and God will shelter them with his presence. The natural problems of a difficult life on earth like hunger, thirst, and labor in the scorching sun will be gone forever, and, in language taken from the beloved Twenty-Third Psalm, God promises He will be in the midst of them as their shepherd, guiding them to springs of living water and wiping away every tear from their eyes. Thus, the reality of human need, suffering, and grief is at once affirmed and ended forever in the life to come.

---

4. Rev 7:14.
5. Isa 1:18.

8

The Seventh Seal and the First Four Trumpets

CHAPTER 8 BEGINS ABRUPTLY; the seventh seal has been opened. The immediate response is silence in all of heaven for about half an hour. In dramatic contrast to all the earlier descriptions of singing and shouts of praise, there is now only sacred, awed silence, the inevitable first response to the *mysterium tremendum et fascinans* ("tremendous and fascinating mystery") of the encounter with the holy, to use Rudolph Otto's phrase. In the silence the angels go to work to do God's bidding. First, the seven angels are given seven trumpets, but they do not sound them yet. Their expectant waiting around the throne is depicted in tapestry thirteen with the angels holding their trumpets away from their mouths. Notice the seven seals on the book; the last seal is still in the forehoof of the Lamb, for he has just opened it.

Then another angel comes to stand at the altar with a golden censer; he is given incense to mingle with the prayers of the saints, and their combined smoke rises before God. The prayers of the saints for the coming of God's kingdom, the petition we make every time we say the prayer Jesus taught us, are actually blended with the incense of heaven to be presented to God. How important then are our prayers! This passage suggests that they are somehow a part of what is necessary for the future to come into being as God has planned it. Somehow our freely offered prayers are all part of His purpose and will. In this beautiful and peaceful tapestry, the fire on the altar is shown supporting the rainbow throne. The censer in the angel's hands seems in motion, its chains slack at the end of its arc, as it captures the flames of the altar of God to be thrown onto the earth.

After this deep silence of praise, the action and the noise begin again. The angel takes fire from the altar with the censer and throws it upon the earth, and lightning, thunder, loud noises, and an earthquake ensue as the seven angels prepare to blow their horns. This tapestry shows the angel pouring out the flames of God's wrath on the earth and the thunderclouds blowing their lightning bolts down as the first angel-trumpeter sounds his horn. Hail and fire mixed with blood come with the blast of the first trumpet, and a third of the earth and the trees, and all the grass, is burned up. John clasps his face in his hand in dismay to see the destruction.

The small fragment we have of the next tapestry shows the dove of peace from Noah's ark finding the olive tree behind the figure of John. This fragment reminds us that God's purpose and God's peace are the background for this and every tapestry, just as they lie behind even the cataclysms of this world to those who believe in the final victory of God over every evil.

With the blast of the second trumpet, a great burning mountain falls into the sea, and a third of the sea becomes blood, with a third of the living creatures of the sea and a third of the ships on the sea destroyed by it. Creation is being undone, trumpet blast by trumpet blast, but only a third of it at a time. As in the days of Noah, God is not utterly destroying what He has made; and as we have seen earlier, if God proceeds by fractions, then destruction will never be total. Tapestry sixteen shows the destruction of a third of the ships on the sea and the terror of the seven sailors as they perish. The flames on the shore represent the burning mountain which falls into the sea. John is shown turning away and veiling his face because it is so dreadful to behold.

When the third angel blows his trumpet, a great star falls from heaven, "blazing like a torch,"[1] on a third of the rivers and on the fountains of water. The name of this fallen star, which probably represents a fallen angel, is Wormwood—*Absinthus* in the Latin and, ironically, *Chernobyl* in Russian. A third of the waters then become bitter and lethal to those who try to drink it. In the next tapestry, the falling star occupies the center of the piece, surrounded by the red streaks of flame from heaven which fall into the water at the bottom to the great consternation of the human figures, who are here almost as large as those of Saint John and the angel.

1. Rev 8:10.

As the prophet Jeremiah proclaimed almost six hundred years before this vision, men in their folly forsake the source of living water, God, and hew out for themselves broken cisterns that cannot hold water. He was trying to show that the false goods of this world cannot nourish us or give us life. Jeremiah also warned that God would give his people wormwood and gall to drink if they turn away from him.² So now the sources of water which evil people have looked to for their sustenance will actually poison them. When the disastrous nuclear accident at Chernobyl in the former Soviet Union took place in 1985, it exposed to all the ordinary citizens of the USSR the corruption, inefficiency, and callous disregard for the safety of the people by the Communist party leaders. Many political observers point to that catastrophe as the beginning of the end of the Soviet regime. We all know that our technology alone cannot save us, and yet we still often look to the work of our own hands, like the people in Jeremiah's day, instead of to the Lord who made us, for our health and salvation.

The consequences of the fourth trumpet are the undoing of the fourth day of creation in Genesis. On that fourth day God created the heavenly bodies "for signs and seasons and for days and years"³ and to rule over the

2. Jer 9:15.
3. Gen 1:14.

day and the night. Now after the blast of the fourth trumpet, a third of the sun, a third of the moon, and a third of the stars are struck, so a third of their light, by day or night, is darkened. This scene is not represented in the tapestries.

Then an eagle appears crying, "Woe, woe, woe to those who dwell upon the earth, at the blasts of the other trumpets which the three angels are about to blow."[4] The eagle was a symbol of imperial Rome, but it is also a symbol of the love and watchcare of God, as he says to His people in Exodus, "I brought you on eagle's wings" through the wilderness.[5] This eagle is a messenger of God, pronouncing woe to the Kingdoms of the earth like the Roman Empire that persecute the faithful of God and worship themselves and their leaders instead of the God who made them. Yet it is also a merciful warning to them to repent before the next disasters come. The eagle dominates the left part of the tapestry with a banner to represent his cries of woe—*Ve*, in the Latin. The city towers and walls are in the act of tumbling down all over the lower section of the piece, their gay blue towers falling into the green grass.

4. Rev 8:13.
5. Exod 19:4.

9

The Fifth and Sixth Trumpets

WHEN THE FIFTH TRUMPET is blown, another star falls from heaven. This star is an angel doing God's will; for he is given the key to the bottomless pit which he then opens. (In the Apocryphal books of Second Esdras and Enoch, an angel called Uriel is in charge of the abyss.) Out of the shaft, smoke arises which darkens the air; then locusts which have the power of scorpions emerge to torment for five months all those men who do not have the seal of God on their foreheads. They are not to kill the people but only to make them wish for death to end their suffering. Perhaps this torture refers to the torment of guilt and suspicion which those who persist in their sins inevitably endure. One thinks of Lady Macbeth in Shakespeare's play walking in her sleep, wringing her hands and ordering, "Out, damned spot! out, I say!" and her husband Macbeth's lament that "all great Neptune's ocean" cannot wash his hands clean of their murderous blood.[1] Their guilt is indeed tormenting them like stings of scorpions.

---

1. Shakespeare, *Macbeth*, act 5, scene 1, line 38; act 2, scene 2, lines 60.

THE FIFTH AND SIXTH TRUMPETS

The locusts look like battle horses, but have human faces, long hair like women, teeth like lions, and tails like scorpions. They wear gold crowns on their heads, iron breastplates, and the noise of their wings is frightening, as indeed the noise of actual locusts is terrifying. Their king, *Abbadon* in Hebrew and *Apollyon* in the Greek—John gives this name in both languages—is God's angel whom He has sent to carry out this plague. His figure, mounted on one of the locusts, dominates this tapestry, which tries to reproduce these strange beasts as closely as possible to the description in the text. As we observed in the introduction, it is difficult to put all these details together in a picture, but the artist does, and the result is terrifying. The star from heaven and the key are suspended under the angel's trumpet over the pit, and the locust army is riding up out of it following their leader.

When the sixth angel blows his trumpet, a voice from the four horns of God's altar commands him to release the four angels who are bound at the river Euphrates. The voice reminds us of the plea of the martyrs under the altar in chapter 6, "How long?" Tapestry twenty depicts them standing on the water readying their weapons to do God's will. They are to kill one-third of mankind and have been waiting for this exact day and hour; they command troops of cavalry to carry out their grim task. The altar with the Book of Life resting on it is shown in the upper right within the clouds with the figure of God beside it. These horses and riders are fantastic, like the locusts in the last scene, but the depiction in the tapestry again faithfully follows the description. The riders have breastplates the color of fire, sapphire, and sulfur; the horses have lion's heads and serpent's tails, and fire, smoke, and sulfur spew forth from their mouths. They wound people with their mouths and tails while their riders use their weapons upon the people they are trampling down. Notice the serpent tail of the "horse" in the left foreground trying to bite something.

As always in this vision, only a fraction of the people or of the earth is to be harmed. Destruction is never total because it is for the purpose of calling the rest to repent. It also is true to human experience that something or someone always remains after even the worst plagues or disasters. But the remnant here does not repent and turn to God. They do not repent of their false worship, of the works of their hands, nor of their murders, immoralities, sorcery, or theft. False worship is here considered as culpable as evil deeds. If one wonders why, John's answer would be that false worship breeds evil deeds because we create false gods in our own image to cover and vindicate our evil desires and exculpate ourselves. The Bible, on the other hand, teaches that God alone is good; therefore, the reason the first commandment is to worship God alone is precisely because God's way is the only sure way to human goodness. All other worship leads to wickedness.

The theme being set forth here is the ancient one of the Hebrew prophets: they foretold destruction if God's people would not return to right worship and righteous deeds. At the same time, however, they always held out hope that if the people would repent, God would spare them. In Revelation, as in the writings of the Hebrew prophets, refusal to repent in the face of disasters and torture redounds to the blame of those who persist in their sin. Like Pharaoh during the plagues of the exodus, if they harden their hearts and do not see the power of God at work in the world, they bring their destruction upon themselves.

10

The Little Scroll

THERE IS NOW AN interlude before the seventh trumpet sounds, heightening the sense of drama and expectancy. An angel wrapped in a cloud with a rainbow over his head comes down from heaven with a scroll open in his hand. This angel is depicted in the left upper corner of the tapestry as he comes down from the presence of God, which is symbolized by the cloud,

THE LITTLE SCROLL

and is seen again on the right side of the tapestry as he stands with one foot in the sea and one the land, symbolically bestriding the whole world, and roaring like a lion. His roaring causes seven thunders to sound, represented by the animal faces in the clouds between them and over John, who is seated and writing it all down. But a voice from heaven tells him not to write it down but to seal up what the thunders have said, just as Daniel was told to seal up his vision.

Perhaps what the thunders have said is now explained by the words of the angel and that is why there is no need for writing it twice. The angel lifts his right hand to swear by the creator of the world that there is to be no more delay. The mystery which God has announced to all his prophets is at last to be fulfilled when the seventh angel blows the seventh blast on the trumpet.

But before that happens, a voice from heaven tells John to take the scroll and eat it, just as Ezekiel was told in his vision to eat the scroll. Once again John is identifying himself with his biblical predecessors. In this tapestry we see the angel giving John the scroll to eat; it is shown, however, as a book. An angel behind him represents the voice from heaven telling him to eat the scroll-book; this angel seems to have helped him stand up and is almost pushing him towards the mighty angel with the book. The other angel is the same one from the previous scene, standing with one foot on the water and one foot upon the land, dominating the scene as a symbol of God's power.

Eating the word of God symbolizes internalizing the message the visionary prophet must later speak. It is also reminiscent of the Christian Eucharist in which we consume the body and blood of Jesus Christ, the Word of God made flesh. The scroll is sweet to the taste because it is the word of God; but it is bitter to his stomach because John must prophesy against many peoples, nations, tongues, and kings. The message he must give will not be welcome because few welcome a call to repentance. Most prefer instead to call the evil they do good and the good preached to them evil, as Isaiah said so long ago. Yet heeding the message to repent is one's only chance to see the glory of God and be a part of His coming kingdom!

11

The Two Martyrs and the Seventh Trumpet

There is a break here between the second and third sets, so the next tapestry is of another "grand personage" reading this book thirteen centuries later. (The one before the second set is missing.) Students of the tapestries call this one "The Doctor"; he reminds us of how important reading and understanding this work was to the people of that time, difficult though it may have been to interpret then as now. The coat of arms on the butterflies behind him are of Louis the First of Anjou, who commissioned this work, and his wife, Marie de Bretagne; the flag which the angel waves at the top is of the arms of Anjou as well. Butterflies are, as we have seen, a symbol of the resurrection of Christ.

Chapter 11 of Revelation begins with the angel giving John a measuring rod with which to measure the temple of God. This represents the new temple of the heavenly city, not the actual temple in Jerusalem, which had been destroyed by the Roman Emperor Titus in AD 66. The command to measure the temple is a way of saying that God has standards by which he judges us, and He instructs His prophets to proclaim those standards to the people. The court outside the temple, however, is not to be measured, for John is told that it will be given over to the nations who will trample all over the holy city for a definite period of time, forty-two months. No matter how bad persecution becomes right now, it will end; the trampling of the infidels will end soon. As we have seen, setting a certain date for the end of this forty-two-month period is a risky business, but giving an exact period of time gives hope. If I think I know when the trials will end, I can hope to last until then.

God has prepared a place for us, as Jesus promised, and this new temple is awaiting our coming. Tapestry twenty-five shows John kneeling at the feet of the angel to receive the measuring rod and his instructions. The angel points to a beautiful Gothic chapel with a tile floor and three, pointed-arch windows looking down on an altar. The chalice and paten, vested for the Eucharist, are on the altar, as well as the candles lit for the mass. One wonders if this is a portrait of an actual chapel that the artist, Jean de Bruges, knew. It certainly seems welcoming, in any case, to one who would worship God now and forever.

John is now told that God is sending two witnesses to earth who will be given power to prophesy for a set period of time—one thousand two hundred and sixty days. They are to be clothed in sackcloth, a sign of mourning, and they are called "two olive trees" and "two lampstands," using the images from the prophet Zechariah again. These witness-prophets are usually identified with Moses and Elijah, for they have powers which recall the powers of Elijah and Moses in their earthly lives. But they also have a larger symbolism—the fact that God has always sent witnesses and prophets to speak his truth to people and is doing so again through John and this vision. In this tapestry one figure is reaching up into heaven to stop the rain from coming down, as Elijah did in the time of Ahab, and the other figure is breathing fiery words onto the people. They are shown again in the same panel both turning water into blood, as Moses did to the Nile during the plagues. Since it was Elijah and Moses who appeared with Jesus in the transfiguration in the Synoptic Gospels, these two prophets are regarded especially as witnesses to the truth of who Jesus really is—the Son of God, the promised Messiah, and now, the Lamb of God who sits upon the throne. These witnesses of the vision, however, do not end their lives as Moses and Elijah did; instead, they share the fate of the Lamb. Once their testimony has been given, the beast that comes up from the bottomless pit makes war upon them, conquers them, and kills them.

The next tapestry shows the attack of this beast. He has killed one prophet, or witness, and is fighting with the other one, who is grabbing the bearded face of his strange mount. This beast is the first of four similar beasts in this book who all together represent the antichrist, or Satan, he who fights and tries to destroy the faithful. If even the famous and successful prophets of the past like Moses and Elijah must suffer and die again if they return to give witness in this last evil time to the truth that Jesus is Lord, how glorious is the company of witnesses which the persecuted Christians are joining in their martyrdom!

All the people of the world who are not followers of Christ rejoice at the deaths of the two witnesses. Their dead bodies are left in the street for three and a half days, and people refuse to allow them to be placed in a tomb, unlike the fate of our Lord. The city is called Sodom, that most wicked of cities in the book of Genesis; but at the same time, it is called Egypt, and also "where their Lord was crucified,"[1] which would be Jerusalem. It seems then that every city is represented here—everywhere that men feel so powerful they do not need the salvation offered by God and kill His prophets at will.

---

1. Rev 11:8.

The idea presented here—that each and every sinful city of this world in every time and place is where Jesus was crucified—is a corollary to the teaching that we ourselves, by our sins, participate in the crucifixion of Christ. Tapestry twenty-eight shows the bodies of the witnesses lying outside a symbolic city as the people make merry and give each other gifts, I suppose, of congratulations! Everyone likes to see the defeat, if not the death, of one who has condemned their ways as sinful and tormented them by preaching judgment. These people have a real party to celebrate the demise of the prophets who pointed out their sin, rejoicing that the witnesses are dead.

But just as Jesus was raised on the third day and then later taken to heaven in a cloud, so these martyrs are resurrected and taken up into heaven. There is an earthquake, as there was at the hour of Jesus's death, and when many of the people who have been rejoicing are killed, the rest, the remnant, in their terror, give glory to God. In the next tapestry the witnesses are shown coming back to life; the doves that are flying in front of their faces represent their spirits returning to them. The voice that tells them to "come up hither" to heaven is the angel on the top right, and their ascent is represented by the cloud at the top left enclosing them, with only the hems of their robes showing. The city is collapsing in the earthquake on the right side of the scene as two people who have survived look on with fear.

Now the second woe has passed, and the stage is set for the third woe, which comes with the seventh trumpet. When the final trumpet sounds, loud voices in heaven cry out the words made so famous in modern times as the text of Handel's "Hallelujah!" chorus from *Messiah*:

> The kingdoms of this world are become the kingdoms of our Lord, and of his Christ; and he shall reign for ever and ever. (Rev 11:15 KJV)

The twenty-four elders on their thrones fall on their faces at this shout of praise and add their song to the paeans, giving thanks to God for taking his power and beginning his reign, the consummation of the prayer of the church, "Thy kingdom come!" They praise God for now destroying those who destroyed his prophets, servants, and saints, and proclaim that the time for the judging the dead has arrived. At this moment God's temple in heaven is opened, showing the ancient ark of the covenant, and thunder, lightning, earthquake, and hail accompany the showing. The ark here represents God's protection of his faithful people, just as the ancient ark protected the Israelites in battle. In the tapestry God in heaven is showing a book that represents the covenant, and the beasts spitting out lightning from their mouths are the thunder. Below on the right the twenty-four elders, crowns of victory on their heads, worship God in a sort of heavenly choir stall.

12

The Woman Clothed with the Sun

THE SECOND HALF OF the book of Revelation begins with another sevenfold scheme of portents of God's coming reign. The first is by far the most famous: the vision of the woman clothed with the sun. Just as the first book of the Bible tells the story of the creation of the world and of the human race, the last book of the Bible retells the story of the birth of the one who will redeem the world. Just as Eve, the mother of all living, occupies the central place in the story of man's fall from paradise, so here another woman, who is at once the symbolic representation of Mary, the mother of Jesus, and of the church, the body of Christ, is at the center of the portent showing how God has saved and will save his chosen people from the forces of evil which seek to destroy them. The seventh trumpet blast which brings in the Kingdom is followed by this portent representing God's plan for the redemption of the world He has made—the birth of Jesus to a woman. Salvation is inexorably set in motion by the birth of the one worthy to open the Book of Life.

Before she appears, however, there is preliminary sign: the temple of God is opened in heaven, and the ark of the covenant again appears. This time, the ark is to remind us of the famous salutation of Elizabeth to Mary in the Gospel of Luke, one which identifies Mary, who is bearing Jesus in her womb, with the ark of the covenant by repeating King David's words when the original ark was brought to his house. David had said, "How can the ark of the LORD come to me?" Elizabeth says, "Who am I that the mother of my Lord should come to me?"[1] Just as the ark contained the old covenant which God gave his people through Moses, Mary contains in her womb Jesus, who is himself the new covenant that fulfills the old. The appearance of the opened ark in heaven, then, is a sign that the woman who appears next is she who bore the new covenant, Mary of Nazareth. As the first believer in God's promise to the world in His son, she is the mother in faith of all who put their trust in Jesus. And since Saint Paul called the church "the body of Christ," she who bore Jesus in her own body becomes by analogy the "mother of the church."

This woman who now appears in heaven is "clothed with the sun"; she has the moon under her feet and a crown of twelve stars upon her head. Whereas gentiles worship the heavenly bodies as deities, they are here seen in their proper place as part of the creation and as adornments for the woman who brings the Savior into the world. The Roman Catholic doctrine of the assumption of Mary into Heaven, and its concomitant idea of Mary crowned as Queen of Heaven, looks to this passage for biblical allusion. It is read at the Feast of the Assumption, August 15, in Roman Catholic, Anglican, and other churches. In this tapestry the fiery rays of the sun surround her crowned head and shoulders, and the hornéd moon at her feet forms a bulwark against the dragon below.

The woman in the vision is first in the anguish of labor pains, in the very act of delivering her male child who is to "rule all the nations with a rod of iron."[2] She has not escaped the "curse" given to Eve, that in pain she will bring forth her children, but rather is in solidarity with all human women who bring new life into the world through the anguish of labor. God intends to save the world through a birth—not some other kind of intervention—and the one who is born is God's son, a sign of His eternal plan for the salvation of the world before all time. As Saint Paul put it, "But when the time had fully come, God sent forth his Son, born of a woman . . . so that we might receive adoption as sons."[3]

But the forces of evil appear immediately. Another portent, a great red dragon appears and stands ready to devour the child as soon as the woman brings him forth. A male child, who will "rule all the nations," is born, but God immediately catches him up into heaven out of the dragon's reach. This portent recalls the story of King Herod who sought to kill the

---

1. 2 Sam 6:9; Luke 1:43.
2. Rev 12:5.
3. Gal 4:4.

Christ-child, trying to trick the wise men into revealing where he was by pretending to want to go and worship him. Evil often uses hypocrisy to attain its ends, and when it is frustrated, like Herod when the wise men went back by another way, it lashes out in terror. Herod killed all the baby boys in Bethlehem in his rage and jealousy of the divine king-child; here the deadly sweep of the dragon's tail pulls down one-third of the stars.

Yet, just as God protected his Son and the woman through Joseph, who, being warned by God in a dream, took Mary and the child into Egypt, so in this portent God prepares a place for the woman in the wilderness into which she flees. In tapestry thirty-one she is seen at rest in the circle of clouds of God's protection, surrounded by angels flying down from heaven, one of whom is reaching out to take the child up to heaven. Since the dragon is described as having ten horns, they are divided four on the highest head and one each on the other six heads. The stars that the dragon is pulling down from heaven are seen above and below his tail, but the twelve stars on her crown are secure.

She is to remain in the wilderness for a set time—one thousand two hundred and sixty days. Now this woman no longer primarily represents Mary of Nazareth but the persecuted church which has struggled to bring the good news of salvation to the world and which is suffering for that endeavor. As we have seen, the fixed number of days is not so much so that people can calculate where we are at any given time relative to the end of time, but to offer hope that this time will indeed end and God knows when. Then the faithful people she represents will be brought out of the wilderness and into the marriage feast of the Lamb; knowing this, they must hold fast to their faith and not give up hope.

The second vision in this series now reveals the unthinkable: war in heaven. The great archangel Michael and his angels fight against the dragon and his angels. As Henry Adams noted in his 1924 work, *Mont St. Michel and Chartres*, all of medieval France was devoted to the virgin Mary and the archangel Michael. Mary is the feminine principle of beauty and peace, home and love; Michael is the masculine principle of warfare and knighthood, courtesy and bravery. In these tapestries woven for the Duke of Anjou, it is fitting that the tapestry of the virgin Mary as Queen of Heaven, resting on her cloud with the dragon below, would hang next to the one of the mighty archangels with his cohorts, victoriously plunging their lances into the throats of the dragon and his assistant dragon. How they must have inspired their original viewers in that time of chivalry and Christendom! This tapestry shows a dramatic contrast between the heavenly angels in their clouds, dominated by the heroic figure of Saint Michael in the middle, and the heavy red dragon and his minion pinned to the ground below them by their lances. Saint Michael's lance is cruciform, reminding us that the victory has already been won by the sacrifice of our Lord on the cross. The angel who is proclaiming the victory is seen leaning out of the cloud to tell Saint John.

But how can there be war in heaven? Don't we conceive of heaven as the one place where God totally rules, and His will is perfectly done? As we pray in the Lord's Prayer, "Thy will be done on earth as it is in heaven." As we discussed in the introduction, one way to interpret the petition in the Lord's Prayer for God's will to be done on earth "as it is" in heaven is that there needs to be peace in heaven as well as in earth, instead of the usual interpretation that there needs to be the same peace on earth that is already enjoyed in heaven. Here at least, there is war in heaven—a seeming contradiction of terms if we think of heaven only as the final place of rest and joy and not as the scene of cosmic power for which angels did battle once upon a time. Milton takes this passage and the mythology which later grew up around it as the basis for the first part of his epic poem *Paradise Lost*, creating a fascinating and almost compelling character out of the rebellious archangel, Satan. We shall see that God will promise a new heaven as well as a new earth in the end of this vision—that will be the place where God's will is always done.

Here, for the first time, the dragon is called the devil, or Satan, thereby identifying him with the accusing angel in the first chapter of the book of Job, as well as Jesus's name for Simon Peter when he tempted him not to suffer, and who entered Judas to cause him to betray his Lord.[4] The exact nature of Satan's evil is also described; he is the deceiver of the whole earth. A major theme of Revelation is that human evil is the result of deception and trickery. We think that power and earthly goods and comforts can make us happy and can save us in the time of trial. We are so mistaken about the nature of truth and goodness because there is a power about that keeps telling us these lies. In a way, we are to be pitied because we are so badly deceived. That is why God keeps offering us signs and portents to show us that it is through faith in the blood of the Lamb—and only by that—that we can find salvation and happiness.

The third vision consists in a loud voice which calls from heaven announcing that "the accuser" has been cast down, fulfilling the vision of Jesus in Luke's Gospel: "I saw Satan fall like lightning from heaven."[5] That is good news; we will not be accused of sin any more, not because we have ceased to sin but because the Lamb has bought our redemption by his own blood. The price has been paid. "Who can bring any charge against God's elect," as Paul says in Romans![6] The fact that the forces of good win here and Satan is cast down from heaven teaches us that good will always win the victory over evil. But the bad news is that Satan and his evil angels are now afoot in the world, angry and frustrated because they know their time is short; the voice pronounces woe upon the earth and sea where the devil will wreak his havoc.

---

4. Matt 16:23; John 13:27.
5. Luke 10:18.
6. Rom 8:33.

In the fourth vision the furious dragon, realizing he has been cast down from heaven, pursues the woman who has borne the male child. She is given eagle's wings to fly away to safety in the wilderness again, reminiscent of the psalmist's longing for the wings of a dove to fly away to the wilderness. Tapestry thirty-three shows her receiving her great green wings from the angel's hand, looking back on the threatening dragon not in fear but with calm confidence. Still, he pursues her, trying to sweep her away with water pouring out of his mouth. She is shown in the next tapestry with red wings, flying through the air as the dragon spews water like vomit from his seven mouths. Here, as in the story of Noah, or the psalm that cries out, "Save me, O God, for the waters have risen up to my neck,"[7] water is the image, not of salvation and life but of death and destruction. The devil has great powers, but they are never enough to win the victory, any more than Herod's evil slaughter of the innocents was able to kill the Word-Made-Flesh. The earth itself comes to her aid, swallowing up the water, as is shown in the bottom of the tapestry. Again, we think of the personification of the earth and natural objects ("O all ye green things, praise ye the Lord"[8]) in the Psalms, and of

7. Ps 69:1.
8. Episcopal Church, Book of Common Prayer, canticle 1.

Jesus saying that if the people did not praise him as he entered into Jerusalem, the stones themselves would sing. All of God's creation is longing for its consummation.

Like the villain in a melodrama saying, "Curses, foiled again," the dragon is angry and frustrated, so he goes off to attack a less formidable target, the rest of the woman's offspring. This time it is not the Holy Child that is endangered, since he has been caught up into heaven, but those who keep the commandments of God and bear testimony to Jesus. So here the woman is clearly seen as the mother of the church, which is converting the world to Christ. This means that Mary the mother of Christ is shown here as the mother of the church, that is, the mother of all faithful people as well. And the faithful are thus identified with Christ himself as his brothers and sisters.

Tapestry thirty-five shows the last verse of the chapter:

> Then the dragon was angry with the woman, and went off to make war on the rest of her offspring, on those who keep the commandments of God and bear testimony to Jesus. And he stood on the sand of the sea. (Rev 12:17)

The devil is standing on the sand of the sea with his back to the water while the offspring of the woman, one of whom is a monk, valiantly fight him. It looks as if the dragon has been mortally wounded and is about to be pushed into the sea. The struggle is not to be over quite so soon, however.

13

Satan's Accomplices: The Second and Third Beasts

The dragon, Satan, is fighting with his back to the sea, but instead of that being a hopeless position, it is the source of new strength. As so often occurs in this life, just when one thinks that evil is about to be vanquished, a new source of it makes an appearance. Thus, in this fifth vision an accomplice of Satan rises out of the sea at his back. This helper is another beast, but it is a combination of leopard, lion, and bear. This beast is nevertheless an imitation of its master, for it too has seven heads and ten horns. He wears his diadems upon his horns and has blasphemous names inscribed on his foreheads. He represents the emperors of Rome, the lackeys and instruments of Satan, who are persecuting the Christians and killing them. One of his heads has a mortal wound which was healed. That is thought to refer to the Emperor Nero, who committed suicide in AD 68 by stabbing himself in the throat. Since there was a rumor that he was not really dead, and a popular belief arose that he would return somehow, Nero, more than any other Roman emperor, was identified with the antichrist who would plague the world before the victorious return of the true Messiah. The term "antichrist," however, is not to be found in Revelation; it is from the first epistle of John: "Children, it is the last hour; and as you have heard that antichrist is coming, so now many antichrists have come; therefore, we know that it is the last hour."[1] (The nineteenth-century German philosopher, Friedrich

---

1. 1 John 2:18.

Nietzsche, made that term well known in his writings, along with his declaration that "God is dead.")

This assistant devil as depicted in the tapestry does not seem as hideous as the dragon, perhaps because the mythical serpentine form of the dragon is more terrifying than the lions' heads we all are familiar with in the real world. But precisely because this beast is not quite so hideous, it can be more dangerous. John warns us of that by telling us that there are blasphemous names written on each forehead, in contrast with the saints who are to be sealed upon their foreheads with the sign of the cross. The third commandment, "Thou shalt not take the name of the LORD thy God in vain; for the LORD will not hold him guiltless, who takes his name in vain,"[2] is one which we often do not take very seriously today. In the time of persecution, however, when calling upon the name of the Lord is one's only hope, those who blaspheme are seen to be in league with the devil and his minions and following their evil example.

Mimicking God, who has given his power and authority to his Son, the Lamb who sits upon the throne, the dragon gives this second beast his authority and power; that is symbolized in this tapestry by the dragon handing his scepter to the beast as he stands, hind legs upon the sea and one foreleg on the ground, like the angel in the previous visions. As Saint Thomas Aquinas reminds us, evil is real but it is not something; that is to say, it has no independent existence on its own but is rather an absence of, or perversion of, the good. So the great dragon Satan can only imitate God and try to deceive his fellow creatures into thinking he has power and glory and thereby pervert God's purposes; he has no creative ability in and of himself, for he is just a creature like the rest of us. Remember the words of Genesis: "Now the serpent was more subtle than any other wild creature that the LORD God had made."[3] Our power to create and to flourish is through the power of the Holy Spirit which lives and works in us; if we cut ourselves off from that Spirit, then, like the beast, we are left with only the ability to parody and obstruct, not create. The beast may have a seal to give his followers, but it is the seal of death, not of life. Furthermore, his assistants, the Roman emperors and other kings of this world, would have no power at all if God had not granted it to them for a time to suit his purposes. As Jesus said to Pilate, "You would have no power over me unless it had been given you from above."[4]

2. Exod 20:7.
3. Gen 3:1.
4. John 19:11.

SATAN'S ACCOMPLICES: THE SECOND AND THIRD BEASTS

In all these visions about the beasts making war upon the faithful, John is encouraging his readers to be like Jesus and trust that, even as they are led away to torture and death, God is working his purpose out through them and will use their sufferings as part of his ultimate victory. Jesus's cruel death was in itself a victory over the forces that rule this world, not just something that was necessary in order for there to be the resurrection. That is a major point of Johannine theology—that the moment of Jesus's glory is the moment when he is lifted up on the cross. Throughout the Gospel of John, Jesus speaks of the time when he will be lifted up and glorified, and he always is referring to his crucifixion. Now the aged John relating his vision is exhorting his readers to stand fast in their refusal to sacrifice to the emperor as a god, and not to compromise with idolatry in any way because a greater glory than this world can offer awaits them even in the hour of their deaths, not just afterwards.

His message is deeply inspiring to those who would follow Jesus in any age: the moment when we must confess our faith in the face of severe penalty and harm is our moment of glory too. Jesus taught his disciples to pray, "Lead us not into temptation, but deliver us from evil," because he knows our weakness, as it says in the psalm. We should pray to be spared the test since we might not be strong enough to endure, and we might betray our Lord, as one of his twelve closest disciples did. But if the temptation, test, and evil are set before us, the story of the three young men in the book of Daniel who are about to be thrown into the fiery furnace should be our inspiration.

In Daniel, which is the source for so much of the imagery and thematic material of Revelation, Shadrach, Meshach, and Abednego are conquered Jews in exile who have been put in high places in King Nebuchadnezzar's court because of their intelligence and diligence. They have no desire to defy the king, but they are faithful in their prayers and practices as Jews. Their envious enemies at court, however, trick the king into pronouncing a death sentence on anyone who does not serve the king's gods and worship the images he has made. They are caught at prayer to the Lord, refuse to worship the king's idols, and thus are brought before him in chains. When the king asks them,

> "If you do not worship, you shall immediately be cast into a burning fiery furnace; and who is the god that will deliver you out of my hands?"
> ... [They reply] "If it be so, our God whom we serve is able to deliver us from the burning fiery furnace; and he will deliver us out of your hand, O king. But if not, be it known to you, O king, that we will not serve your gods or worship the golden images which you have set up." (Dan 3:15, 17–18)

"But if not" is the key phrase; for although the saints pray and wait in hope for God's vindication and rescue, they know full well that many of them have not been and probably will not be delivered from the furnace, the lash, the prison cell, or the cross. John, furthermore, claims that there is hope even if "but if not" occurs and they are not delivered from death. This is true firstly because our faithfulness and endurance will be our moment of glory and secondly because these terrible events are part of what must happen before the reign of God comes to pass. In a way, one's martyrdom is helping bring about the coming of the Kingdom.

SATAN'S ACCOMPLICES: THE SECOND AND THIRD BEASTS

But until that time, most men do not understand the truth that Jesus is Lord, and they continue to worship the beast and his co-beast. The tapestry shows the people of the world in reverent worship before both beasts; the assistant beast holds the scepter while the first beast commands the adoration of the people. The next tapestry shows people kneeling before the second beast with his scepter while the dragon is in the background, looking both ways with his many heads as if to protect his protégé. The people adore the beast and say, "Who is like the beast, and who can fight against it?"[5] That is a parody of the name of the archangel Michael, who had cast the first beast down from heaven. *Mi-cha-el* in Hebrew translates, "Who is like God?" And Michael's name derives from the praises of God by Moses in his song after the exodus:

> Who is like thee, O LORD, among the gods?
> Who is like thee, majestic, in holiness,
> terrible in glorious deeds, doing wonders?
> (Exod 15:11)

Again, we see that evil must parody good, for it is not some *thing* and so cannot create anything by itself, not even songs of praise.

5. Rev 13:4.

The Last Word

The very fact that evil seems to be regnant means that the end is getting close. We know from our own experience that sometimes things have to get worse before they get better, for the horror of evil has to be made plain before good can begin to triumph. When evil presents itself in a dreadful and unthinkably horrible way, however, then good people sacrifice even their lives to stop it. One thinks of September 11, 2001, when the Al Qaeda hijackers flew three planes into the World Trade Center and the Pentagon. Once the passengers on the fourth hijacked plane heard the news on their cell phones and realized the extent of the evil these people were doing, they overpowered the hijackers and took their plane down, causing their own immediate deaths but sparing those in the next targeted building. That was a self-sacrificing triumph of human goodness brought about by the recognition of the horrible evil at hand.

At this point the third set of tapestries ends, and there is a piece of another grand person reading the book, reminding the viewers again of the importance of studying the word of God. There are elaborate flowers in the background here as well as the butterflies seen in the other ones that have survived. This man has a turban of sorts wrapped on the top of his head and is reading the book from a bookstand.

In the sixth vision of this series, John says that the blasphemous beast is allowed to exercise authority for a fixed period of time—forty-two months. During this time, it is allowed to make war on the saints, conquer them, and then have authority over every tribe and people. "Everyone" will worship it. Only those whose names are written in the Book of Life will have the courage and faith to be like the three young men facing the furnace and refuse to worship evil. "Here is a call for the endurance [and faith] of the saints," writes John.[6] In this tapestry the people shown are still worshiping the beast. But we see Christ in the clouds of heaven in the upper right to remind us that it is he who reigns, not the beast, who only pretends to.

The seventh vision is of yet another beast, one arising out of the earth. Again, the message is that evil can appear anywhere at any time—out of the earth as well as out of the mysterious deep, or even falling down from heaven itself. This beast has two horns like a lamb, so it resembles the Lamb of God and can therefore deceive men more readily. Here it is shown sitting on a throne with the scepter in its hand and something like a Roman toga draped to reveal a muscular, human-shaped body below his rather noble-looking lion's head. It is much more attractive than the second beast, which

6. Rev 13:10.

now stands in front of him. But it speaks like its master, the dragon. Jesus warned his disciples, "False Christs and false prophets will arise and show signs and wonders, to lead astray, if possible, the elect."[7] This beast mimics the miracles of Jesus and the prophets, even making fire come down from heaven as the great Elijah did. In this tapestry the second beast with seven lion's heads guards him while he uses his scepter to make fire appear in the clouds on the top right. The amazed people below the fire are kneeling to worship him.

As we have seen, although the term is not used in Revelation, this beast is usually identified as the "false Christ" or "antichrist" since his aim is to deceive people into thinking he is the true Messiah, as both Jesus and then John warned. Its appearance highlights an important theme of this vision: the forces of evil meet with success by deceiving people into thinking they are good. To a great extent then, people who worship the beast are deceived; they are not guilty of sinning with malice so much as ignorance. They are easily led, like silly sheep going astray after a false shepherd. God

7. Mark 13:22.

has revealed the truth to his prophets and seers like John so that they may tell us the truth about good and evil. We need to heed them precisely because the truth is not necessarily obvious to us, deceived by appearances as we so often are.

Tapestry forty-one illustrates the next passage which says that he also functions as a priest of the devil, for he leads the people to worship the second beast. He is able to make the image of that beast speak and to enforce the death penalty against those who refuse to worship the image. The beast on a vested altar has flames coming forth from its mouth to represent his false speech. Those who give in and worship the image of the beast are safe, while those who refuse are depicted on the right, near the hem of John's robe, being put to the sword. Specifically, John is referring to the cult of the emperor of Rome here. Christians who refused to burn incense before the statue of the emperor as *kyrios*, or Lord—the title reserved in Scripture for God Himself and now also for Jesus the Christ—were imprisoned or executed. John's vision is encouraging Christians not to give in and do it. "Maybe you will be executed too; but, whatever the cost, be like the three young men in the book of Daniel and say, 'But if not, we will step into the fire anyway!'" That is his message.

SATAN'S ACCOMPLICES: THE SECOND AND THIRD BEASTS

This puppet beast, that first and foremost represents the authority and power of Rome, is next shown on his throne marking everyone on the right hand or forehead so that no one can buy or sell unless he has the mark of the beast. This kingly beast controls commerce and trade; the invisible mark of baptism which identifies the saints is parodied by the mark of those who put their trust in buying and selling. The beast looks munificent as he puts his mark on the people surrounding his throne. Two men come from afar on horseback and one on foot to receive his imprimatur, thinking they are lucky to get it. In the last three tapestries John is seen standing in his portico, observing with his book in his hand; but in this scene he has opened the book as if to consult it.

In one of the most famous passages in Revelation, John is now told that the mark of the beast is an earthly number—666. What is the meaning of this number, so familiar to viewers of devil-horror movies today? Since seven—as the number of heaven (three) plus the number of earth (four)—symbolizes perfection, six falls short of perfection. The first idea is that the devil can only attempt to be like God but cannot ever quite make it. More importantly, however, the ancient practice of "gematria," or using the number for each letter of the alphabet as a symbolic representation of a name to make riddles and ciphers, is almost certainly involved in this number for the beast. In Latin, certain letters and combinations of them were used for numbers; even though we have used Arabic numerals for arithmetic for many centuries, we are all familiar with Roman numerals. But in the Hebrew and the Greek languages, each letter of the alphabet was also a sign for a number, so any name could be expressed as a group of numbers or, more obscurely, as a sum of numbers. Since the Old Testament was written in Hebrew and the New Testament in Greek, the symbolism of numbers and letters can legitimately be applied in both, where appropriate, to interpret symbolic meanings in the texts.

Six hundred and sixty-six, most scholars agree, is most likely to represent Nero Caesar, who had tortured and executed the Christians of Rome in AD 60 and later committed suicide, as we have seen. But this number also refers to all the emperors of Rome, who all took the name of "Caesar," the name of the great Julius and his adopted son Octavian, who was the first "emperor." The seven heads on the beast can each represent one of them, as well as all those in positions of power who have persecuted Christians. John is saying quite plainly that they all are servants of the beast; they are in league with the devil and his minions. To John's way of thinking, one must choose to be either a servant of God and his Christ or a servant of Satan and his beast. Jesus said, "He that is not against us is for us";[8] John is turning that around to say, "He that is not for us is against us." One must choose sides and not be deceived by what the culture around is saying is all right. It is a matter of eternal life or death!

---

8. Mark 9:40.

14

The Lamb on Mount Zion and His Worshipers

THE NEXT VISIONS GIVEN to John are in dramatic contrast to what he has just seen. Lest faithful people be discouraged by the visions of the beasts and all the people worshiping them, seven visions now begin to reveal what is really happening in the reign of God—a reign which has already begun even though most people do not realize it. First there is a vision of the pure and holy Lamb. Juxtaposed against the scenes of the dragon and the beasts from the sea and the land, he seems so defenseless against these monsters; yet he stands firmly and serenely upon the eternal Mount Zion. In the next tapestry, the Lamb seems to be both in heaven and on earth, for he is standing atop an earthly green mountain with his head and shoulders in the firmament of heaven. This reminds us that Jesus promised his disciples at the moment of his ascension into heaven, "Lo, I am with you always, to the close of the age."[1] The four Gospel writers, represented as always by the creatures from Ezekiel's oracles, are shown in heaven with angels giving testimony to the Lamb.

---

1. Matt 28:20.

With the Lamb on the mountain here on earth are 144,000 faithful people who have his and the Father's name written on their foreheads. Again, this is a vivid contrast with the previous scene of those who have the number of the beast on their foreheads. The number of these saints, twelve times twelve, is a repetition of the number of the martyrs who were sealed in chapter 7, so perhaps these are meant to be the same people. Whether or not they are the same group, 144,000 represents not that particular number of faithful people who have this seal, but some exact number known to God alone. He knows each one who will endure to the end by name. There are no anonymous Christians in God's eyes; he who knows the fall of a sparrow knows each one of his own children, no matter how alone and forlorn one may feel at any given moment. This fixed number of faithful people is represented in the tapestry by the seven men and women who are praying beside the mountain at the feet of the Lamb. Notice the crosses on their foreheads. These look like the Greek letter *tau*, or the Roman capital *T*, but they are crosses, just without the top piece that we usually see in Western art. The ineffable name of God and the holy name of Jesus can be expressed with a single letter when that letter represents the cross!

THE LAMB ON MOUNT ZION AND HIS WORSHIPERS

Then a voice from heaven cries out like the sound of many waters, and thunder and the music of harpers playing accompanies all the saints as they sing a new song before the throne. The elders are shown seated on earth in the previous tapestry, but in the next one we see them in Heaven with the Lamb and the four creatures. In this scene the throne upon the rainbow is empty, suggesting that it is God himself who is seated thereon. The seven faithful people are shown on the right, singing a new song to the Lamb. John tells us that the 144,000 are worthy to learn the new song because they are virgins who have not defiled themselves with women. These faithful people are also called pure because they have not told any lies. Remember that Satan is the great deceiver and the father of lies. It is the truth that shall make us free, as Jesus promised, so being truth-tellers is crucial for all who would follow Jesus.

The praising of virginity, or chastity, here is very interesting in terms of the history of the church. Since Peter himself was married, as were most of the disciples and apostles, virginity is surely being used here not literally in a biological sense but metaphorically, to contrast with fornication and adultery, which refer not only to sexual sins but symbolically to worshiping false gods. Extending this metaphor, the virgin daughter of Jerusalem or the chaste wife was a recurring image in the Hebrew prophets of a people true and faithful to the one God, their Lord. The exaltation of virginity and/or a life of celibacy comes into Christian piety only after New Testament times, as people tried to imitate Jesus and then Saint Paul, who thought the Kingdom was coming so soon that there was no need for a Christian to marry or to desire to. He did say, however, to his fellow Christians that "it is better to marry than to be aflame with passion."[2] The idea was to remain celibate for the sake of service to the faith, both to avoid the cares and temptations of this world and also as a sign of living now in the Kingdom of God, where "there will be no marrying and giving in marriage."[3] But here the virgin is supposed to become a bride, the bride of Christ, so we know we are dealing with a symbol of religious purity, not the fact of sexual abstinence. The imagery of the great whore, or harlot, set over against the virgin bride becomes an important theme as this vision reaches its climax and conclusion.

The next three visions are of angels in mid-heaven who come with messages to all nations, tribes, and peoples. In contrast to the eagle that

2. 1 Cor 7:9.
3. Matt 22:30.

cried out the three "woes" in chapter 8, these angels are bringing good news. The first brings the message to fear God and give Him glory because the hour of judgment has come. He is shown in this tapestry above the men who seem to be discussing the meaning of this message among themselves. The second announces that "Babylon" has fallen. Babylon is the city of the conquest and exile of Judea in the sixth century BC that John now uses to symbolize imperial Rome and all the evil powers of this world. The next tapestry has a very dark blue background with the angel in a cloud showing the scroll with his message to John. Babylon is depicted as a stylized medieval city with towers and houses on its walls, crumbling and falling in on itself.

The third angel proclaims in a loud voice that those who worship the beast and its image, who are marked with his mark, will drink the wine of God's wrath. The beast has imitated the seal of baptism by marking his followers with his seal, the number 666. But that seal will be a seal of doom. Similarly, the wine which God gives us in communion to be the saving blood of Christ for those who bear the mark of true baptism, is now the image of God's wrath for all infidels. The two great sacraments of the church are thus turned around here; what is saving for the faithful is damning for the unfaithful. Their seal and their cup will bring them torment. In the next tapestry the golden chalice for the true blood of Christ stands in the center on the hill behind the victorious Lamb. This is one of the most expressive of the tableaux in the series—notice the facial expression and the hand gestures of the men and the angels listening to these tidings. This fourth vision ends with the writer reminding his readers to endure and keep the faith.

Then the fifth vision appears: a voice from heaven pronounces, "Blessed are the dead who die in the Lord henceforth."[4] "Henceforth" refers to the new age which is dawning and a new blessedness as we realize that there is really just one world which encompasses both sides of the grave and that Jesus is the Lord of both. Then the Spirit Himself replies to give assurance and a promise: "Blessed indeed . . . that they may rest from their labors, for their deeds follow them."[5] This blessing by the Spirit implies that we must keep on laboring until the very end of our lives, never growing

4. Rev 14:13.
5. Rev 14:13.

"weary in well-doing."[6] But it also assures us that our deeds are not in vain; because God knows them, their significance is eternal.

Now sometimes that is interpreted as a Pelagian doctrine, teaching that our good deeds somehow earn us the right to heaven. (Pelagius was a fifth-century Christian heretic who taught just that.) But that is not what is meant. It is our faith and trust in the Lamb That Was Slain that grants us a place among the blessed. But what we do in our lives matters because what Jesus did in his life mattered. By taking on our flesh, the Son of God forever dignified the work of human hands and minds. And furthermore, because it is in this life that we meet our Lord and either choose to follow him or not, the deeds of this life are part of God's eternal plan for the salvation of the world. That is why our good and faithful deeds follow us to heaven where they will be perfected by God into "jewels in our crowns."

The tapestry illustrating this promise is charming. Below are seven grown, bearded men peacefully sleeping together in their beds, four in one and three in another, hands pressed together in prayer—a depiction of a truly blessed death, as the Book of Common Prayer puts it, "Without suffering and without reproach."[7] Above them their souls are being taken up into heaven by angels holding a white drape. And their souls look youthful; there are no beards, and their hair is short and curly. Our souls, like our good deeds, will be restored to the beauty God intended for them, in spite of the wounds and natural decay of living in this fallen world. John is seen here seated and writing all this down on his scroll.

---

6. Gal 6:9.

7. Episcopal Church, Book of Common Prayer, 385.

The sixth vision is of "one like a son of man" seated on a cloud with a crown on his head and a sharp sickle in his hand. We recognize from this description that this must be the victorious Christ at his Second Advent. When an angel tells him the hour has come, he swings his sickle on the earth and reaps it. In this tapestry Christ is shown on a throne in the clouds and again in the fields as the crowned harvester. The harvest is a joyous time in earthly lives, the culmination of the hard work of sowing and growing. The harvest here, as in the parables of Jesus, is a symbol of culmination of life for the faithful; Christ is their recompense and their reward. Happy are those who are gathered in his arms!

The seventh vision, however, shows the other side of the final harvest. Now that Christ has reaped the righteous, who are represented as grain, the angel who has power over fire is instructed to reap the vineyards, which represent the wicked: "Put in your sickle and gather the clusters of the vine of the earth,"[8] says the heavenly voice, echoing the prophet Joel:

> Put in the sickle
> for the harvest is ripe.
> Go in, tread,
> for the wine press is full.
> The vats overflow,
> for their wickedness is great.
> (Joel 3:13)

In this tapestry the angel in the temple of heaven is handing the sickle to the angel on earth, who stands before an altar with a ciborium upon it, the flames for burning the vines at his feet. There is a sense of urgency conveyed by the first angel's face and his pointed finger. A single grapevine, loaded with very ripe grapes, is on a trellis in the center, looking very lovely indeed for a symbol of evil. But the grapevine carefully splayed on the trellis represents all the plots and devices of human wickedness.

8. Rev 14:8.

Whereas God's wrath against an individual sinner can be contained in a single cup, as we saw in verse 10, His wrath against all sinners at the day of judgment results in a huge, overflowing river of blood flowing from the winepress, as high as a horse's bridle for about two hundred miles around the outside of the city. But the source of the blood is sinners' own evil and impious ways. The words of Julia Ward Howe's "Battle Hymn of the Republic" (1862) reflect this same theme: "Mine eyes have seen the glory of the coming of the Lord, He is trampling out the vintage where the grapes of wrath are stored."

The next tapestry illustrates the conclusion of this vision when the angel has cut the grapes of wrath and trodden the winepress. The artist includes the horses with their bridles coming out of the city gates and has added a devil seated on the side of the winepress to make it clear that this *cuvé*, or harvesting of grapes, is of evil. The city must be Jerusalem, for it was outside of the walls of Jerusalem that the blood of Jesus flowed on Golgotha.

THE LAMB ON MOUNT ZION AND HIS WORSHIPERS

The prophecy that there will be such a final harvest is usually interpreted as a separation of the just and faithful from the unjust and unfaithful. The good grain is brought into the heavenly city while the evil grapes are turned to blood outside its walls. But it is also an allegory of the individual soul; and perhaps therein lies its most profound significance. What is there in each of us that deserves to be gathered into the bosom of Christ and made a part of God's eternal kingdom? And what is there in each of us that deserves to die, to be trodden underfoot outside the city, so that one may enter eternal life purified? What in my life will be brought to fulfillment in God's eternal plan, and what will need to come to an end because it glorifies myself instead of God? These are the enduring and universal questions a Christian should ask in contemplating the final judgment, rather than trying to decide which persons are "good grain" and which are "evil grapes of wrath."

15

Seven Angels and Seven Plagues

Now John sees another portent in heaven, seven angels with seven "last" plagues, and another series of sevens begins. The tapestry shows these angels in the clouds of heaven, with the plagues contained in golden flasks that look like liturgical vessels. Below these angels are seven more standing on a sea of glass mingled with fire, playing their harps and singing one of the many hymns of this vision:

> Great and wonderful are thy deeds,
> O Lord God the Almighty!
> Just and true are thy ways,
> O King of the ages!
> Who shall not fear and glorify thy name, O Lord?
> For thou alone art holy,
> All nations shall come and worship thee,
> For thy judgments have been revealed.
> (Rev 15:3-4)

The glassy sea with fire recalls the waters of baptism and the fire of charity. This is a scene of a heavenly liturgy; the angels are praising God for his justice and prophesying that all nations shall come to worship the one God in the end. The plagues the first angels are about to release upon the earth are for the purpose of bringing the nations to a realization of God's judgments so that they can rely on His mercy. "The harps of God"[1] which the angels play are depicted in the tapestry without any strings in some cases—it seems a strange omission.

---

1. Rev 15:2.

The Last Word

   At this point this set of tapestries ends and a new one begins. As is the case with each series of tapestries, it is introduced by a large figure of a grand person reading the book, seated in an elaborate reading desk, guarded from above by angels with banners. This person is dressed in red and blue, and butterflies adorn the background. The sequence resumes with tapestry fifty-five showing the "tent of witness" in heaven opened, as described in verse

5, and the angels coming out of the temple clothed in "pure bright linen," golden girdles around their breasts. The region of heaven is a full semicircle here, and the angels are processing in liturgical fashion towards one of the four living creatures as if they were offering an oblation. The creature shown in the tapestry is the lion, the symbol for the evangelist Saint Mark. Since the lion is the fiercest of the four creatures (the others being the eagle, the ox, and one like a man), perhaps he is the appropriate one to be giving the angels seven golden bowls full of the wrath of God. (One who has read C. S. Lewis's Chronicles of Narnia, however, cannot help but look on this stately lion and see Aslan, the symbol for Christ himself. Maybe Lewis had seen these tapestries before he wrote his books!) The feet standing on the orb over their heads symbolize Christ, the ascended Lord, who rules over all the world even though his presence is hidden from mortal sight.

When the angels receive the bowls full of the wrath of God from the hands of the four creatures, smoke fills the temple. Smoke and cloud are symbols in the Bible of the presence of God and of his power. From Abraham's first covenant, to the cloud by day and pillar of fire by night that guided the tribes of Israel in the wilderness, to the vision of Isaiah when the house was filled with smoke, to the cloud in which Jesus was taken up to heaven at the ascension, cloud and smoke convey the presence of the Almighty in our midst. John is told that no one can enter the temple until the seven plagues are released. God's purposes must be accomplished in His good time, and the message here is that the time has finally come. If the plagues come, then entering the temple will again be possible and very soon. And then, at last, as the angels' song predicts, "All nations shall come and worship thee."

16

The Seven Bowls Poured Out

JOHN THEN HEARS A loud voice—there can be no mistake about what is being said from heaven in John's entire vision because the voice of God's angel is always described as "loud." Here the voice tells the angels to go and pour out their bowls of wrath on the earth. The tapestry which illustrates this scene is particularly beautiful, with four of the angels clustered in the center on the green earth, their pink, gold, and green wings clustered together against the deep blue background. The angel with the loud voice is shown in the heavenly temple calling down to them. The plague from the first bowl is falling down on bare earth at the feet of men who bore the mark of the beast. It will afflict them with foul sores.

The second angel pours his bowl of wrath into the sea and the third angel pours his into the fountains and rivers. The red background of the next tapestry is very appropriate here since the bowl of wrath turns the sea into blood, and every living thing in the sea is killed. One can see them drowning in the foreground. Then all the other sources of water are turned to blood also, recalling the second plague of the exodus when the Nile was turned to blood. The angel of water, shown on the right in the tapestry standing behind an altar with a chalice for the blood of the Lamb on it, speaks of God's justice, "For men have shed the blood of saints and prophets, and thou hast given them blood to drink. It is their due."[1] The double significance of blood is the point here: the blood of the Lamb saves those who trust in it and drink it in the mystery of the Eucharist; but those who shed the blood of the martyrs, described here as drinking it, are poisoned by that blood. The altar, perhaps representing the saints in chapter 6 who lie buried under the altar awaiting God's vengeance, replies, "Yea . . . true and just are thy judgments."[2]

1. Rev 16:6.
2. Rev 16:7.

Creation is being judged and found wanting: first the earth, then the seas and rivers, and now the sun. The fourth angel empties his bowl on the sun and, instead of being darkened as it was when the fourth trumpet sounded, it is allowed to scorch men with fire. So life-giving water has been turned to blood, and now the life-giving sun turns into a torturer. Only a fragment of tapestry sixty survives, but in it one can see the dramatic rays of the sun licking down towards earth and the agony of the people being scorched. The purpose of these plagues, just as with the plagues of the exodus, is to make men realize that the Lord is God and to cause them to turn to Him in repentance and belief. But just as the pharaoh's heart was hardened by the plagues visited upon the Egyptians, the people who are scorched curse God instead of repenting and giving Him glory.

The fifth bowl of wrath has a similar result. When it is poured over the throne of the beast, it brings darkness to the kingdom of the beast. The men gnaw their tongues in anguish, but they curse God and do not repent. The sixth angel pours his bowl on the river Euphrates and dries up its water; evidently it had not previously been turned to blood. There is no concern about being literally consistent here—these portents are symbols of God using everything possible to bring humanity to their senses. Drying up the

Euphrates recalls the dry passage across the Red Sea for the Israelites; it is to prepare the way for the "kings of the east," much as the sixth trumpet called for the locust-horses and riders who would kill one-third of mankind. But these kings are to make war upon the kingdom of the beast to free those who are enslaved by it.

The angel in the tapestry with the fifth bowl is in the center, pouring it out upon the empty altar of the beast. Where has this beast gone? Human figures are shown writhing in agony on the mountainside in the background with the scorching sun still sending its flames down upon them. The angel with the sixth bowl is on the right, and the drying-up river extends from his robes like a train, stopping at the figure of the king on horseback who is coming as summoned.

The beasts appear in the next verse, and in this tapestry they are shown in a defiant pose, arrayed against the lone figure of John as if to threaten him. The dragon is on the back of the beast that arose from the sea, and the second beast who looked so attractive, almost like a lamb when he was set up on the pedestal to be worshiped, now reveals his true hideous visage. John sees three foul spirits like frogs issuing from the mouth of the third beast, the false prophet, and says that these demonic spirits are going abroad mimicking the holy spirits of God by performing signs and gathering the kings of the earth together.

The theme of evil as deception is set forth again. Just because a spirit performs wonders does not mean that it possesses true power; all power comes from God, and God in the end will triumph over those who pervert His power for evil purposes. John interrupts his vision here with a blessing from the Lord himself, recalling the words of Jesus from the Gospels in various places, "Lo, I am coming like a thief! Blessed is he who is awake, keeping his garments that he may not go naked and be seen exposed!"[3] The message is that the battle is coming very soon, and although the faithful may be afraid, they must be prepared. They are to be assembled at a place called *Armageddon* in Hebrew. The name is generally thought to refer to the ancient city of Megiddo, the scene of many important battles, but it has come to stand for a final battle between good and evil.

As the seventh angel pours his bowl of wrath into the air, a great voice sounds out of the temple from the throne saying, "It is done."[4] Flashes of

3. Rev 16:15.
4. Rev 16:17.

lightning and peals of thunder accompany this pronouncement, and an earthquake splits the great city into three parts. Babylon must drink the cup of God's wrath. Islands disappear, and mountains are leveled; wherever the bowl is thrown, the air yields hailstones. But still, human beings do not repent and turn to God; in their pride they remain defiant like the evil beasts and curse God instead of asking for forgiveness.

Christ is shown here with the heavenly city on both sides of him within the cloud at the top, thus identifying him as the source of the voice. It shows the earthly city in pieces, crushing people all around as it falls, with hailstones like large rocks falling amid the ruins. The beast-like faces in the clouds of heaven vomiting down flames represent the thunder and lightning. The cup of the fury of God's wrath is seen in the right center, pouring out blood on the blue rooftops of the collapsing city. Although the Scripture says it is split into three parts, the scene of destruction in the tapestry is more random, with the great hailstones lying around at the bottom of the piece. This is not, however, the final destruction but only a prelude to the final battle; in the tradition of the plagues in the exodus, there will be yet another great cataclysm.

17

The Great Whore

Here begins a series of seven visions of the fall of Babylon, to be followed by seven visions of the beginning of God's eternal reign. This last section of the Revelation to John could be called "A Tale of Two Cities," like Charles Dickens's great novel, for John is shown two cities, one that represents the reign of evil and one that represents the reign of God. These cities are symbolized by two women, one a harlot and one a pure bride brought to her wedding feast, so it could also be called "A Tale of Two Women."

One of the seven angels who had a bowl of wrath invites John to "come," as he is invited so often in this vision, so that he can "show [him] the judgment of the great harlot who is seated upon many waters."[1] The kings of the earth have committed fornication with her and the wine of that fornication has made the dwellers of the earth drunk. Once again, worshiping false gods is described as adultery or fornication. Ordinary people follow the example of their kings and leaders and have gotten drunk on the wine that is the result of their sin. John is shown being led out of his small and safe temple by the angel, who takes his hand to lead him out to marvel at this beautiful woman seated seductively on the third of four terraces bounded by waters. A lovely flowering tree on the right completes the scene of a garden. She is combing her long flowing hair with a rectangular comb typical of those used by the ladies of the fourteenth century, and she is looking at her reflection in a mirror, where her face is clearly woven into the tapestry. Her breasts show through her dress, and she looks very alluring

1. Rev 17:1.

indeed. The letter *Y* in the blue background symbolizes virtue and vice and life and death in medieval iconography. We have seen them on the backs of the elaborate chairs where the grand persons in the tapestries that begin each series sit.

The angel then transports John to the wilderness; in the next tapestry the angel is carrying him in his arms as if he needs protection, and his small cubicle stands empty. The garden scene in the previous tapestry reminds us of Eden, where evil lurked to tempt the first woman and man. So also does the wilderness hold both good and evil. In Rev 12, the woman with the child was taken to the wilderness to be protected and nourished by God for a set time, as shown in tapestry thirty-one. But now the wilderness is the location of the whore seated upon the beast. This tapestry has a red background which links it visually to that other one; but unlike the first one, there is no heaven here. Whereas the woman clothed with the sun and her child are safely ensconced above the clouds where the dragon cannot reach them, this other woman is riding upon the beast with seven heads that is firmly rooted to the green earth under its feet. Evil is very much alive and active here on earth, whether in a cultivated garden or in the wilderness.

The Last Word

The beast with seven heads and ten horns full of blasphemous names is the same one which appeared from the sea in Rev 13, the one to which the dragon gave his power. Here again we see how important it is to denounce blasphemy. The commandment not to take the name of the Lord in vain is not a prohibition against impolite or offensive swearing but rather is intimately connected to fidelity or apostasy; it is a matter of identity. As Saint Paul says, no one can say, "Jesus is Lord" except by the power of the Spirit, so no one who curses Jesus can be one of his own. In a time when Christians were being asked to do just that to save their lives, or else refuse to do that and die, "mere" words which come out of our mouths have eternal significance. Thus, the beast is full of blasphemous names, and the whore has a name of mystery on her forehead that condemns her: "Babylon the great, mother of harlots and of earth's abominations."[2] She is richly adorned with jewels and holds in her hand a cup, a symbol that can be for good or evil in this vision. Her cup, however, is full of abominations and impurities of her fornication; she is drunk with the blood of the saints and martyrs.

2. Rev 17:5.

John marvels at the mystery of the woman and the beast, and the angel explains to him what the beast's fate will be. It will ascend from the bottomless pit and go to perdition, taking with him all those whose names are not written in the Book of Life. The seven heads stand for seven hills; the beast stands for Rome with its seven hills and the seven ancient kings of Rome. The ten horns represent ten kings who will make war on the Lamb. But the Lamb is King of Kings and will conquer them. As for the harlot, the beast will turn on her and hate her; he will devour her and burn her up with fire. There is no mercy among the beasts and their minions—not even for each other—for mercy is from God. Finally, the angel explains that the woman represents Babylon, the evil city of the conquest and exile in the Old Testament, and Rome, the evil city of imperial power and persecution in the New Testament.

18

Visions of the Fall of Babylon: A Tale of Two Cities

THE TALE OF THE evil city in this "Tale of Two Cities" continues with another vision of the fall of Babylon, the ancient city which stands for the contemporary imperial city of Rome and which is symbolized by the harlot who rides upon the beast and sits upon many waters. A bright and splendid angel comes down from heaven to sing a dirge, or one might say a taunt, over the fallen whore, Babylon, mixing the metaphors of woman and city into a powerful image of giving and receiving pollution:

> Fallen, fallen is Babylon the great!
> it has become a dwelling place of demons,
> a haunt of every foul spirit,
> a haunt of every foul and hateful bird;
> for all nations have drunk the wine of her impure passion,
> the kings of the earth have committed fornication with her,
> and the merchants of the earth have grown rich with the wealth of her wantonness.
> (Rev 18:2–3)

This dirge is reminiscent of the book of Lamentations, which bewails the fall of Jerusalem to the Babylonians in 597 BC, describing that city as a bereft and forsaken woman. In this tapestry we see a scene similar to the pouring of the seventh cup upon the city in Rev 16, except this time the foul birds fly above the crumbling walls attacking the hideous demons that are trapped in the wreckage. Saint John has returned to his safe cubicle to observe the destruction.

The angel in the next passage, the fourth vision of the fall of the city, calls for the people in the city to flee "lest [they] take part in her sins."[1] The tapestry shows frightened people heeding the warning of the second angel at the top right of the scene, warning the people not to suffer the city's fate. Her retribution will be double for all the evil she has done, and a double draught of the cup of wrath which she herself has mixed. Shakespeare creates a similar double irony in the final scene of *Hamlet* when the doomed prince, who has been cut with a poisoned rapier, not only stabs his evil stepfather and uncle, King Claudius, with that rapier but also then forces him to drink off the rest of the poisoned cup he had prepared for Hamlet, but which his beloved Queen Gertrude drank by mistake. Laertes, who is dying by the very poison he and the king conspired to put on his rapier to kill Hamlet, cries, "He is justly served; / It is a poison temper'd by himself."[2] The great whore here likewise gets all of the evil she prepared for others, and gets it double. "Overkill" is justice for anyone who has led others astray. As Jesus said, woe unto one by whom another has been led into sin, "It would be better for a

---

1. Rev 18:4.
2. Shakespeare, *Hamlet*, act 5, scene 2, line 323-24.

millstone were hung round his neck and he were cast into the sea, than that he should cause one of these little ones to sin."[3]

The angel goes on to predict that the kings of the earth who committed fornication with the whore will weep and wail as they see the smoke of her burning and say,

> Alas! Alas! thou great city,
> thou mighty city Babylon!
> In one hour has thy judgment come.
> (Rev 18:10)

The merchants of the earth will also weep for her since no one can buy and sell their luxuries. It is important to note that all these luxurious items will be found again in the heavenly city. The beautiful riches of this world are not evil, for they are God's creation wrought by human hands into things of beauty. What is evil is serving them instead of God, the Creator. At the climactic end of the list of things one could buy in the city is the one inherently evil object of ancient trade: "slaves, that is, human souls."[4]

Buying and selling "human souls" was the mainstay of the economic system of the Roman world, and this is one of the few passages in the Bible that speaks of slavery as evil in itself. As recently as the middle of the nineteenth century in the American South, Christians used the letter of Paul to Philemon to argue that the New Testament does not object to slavery; but they were oblivious to or avoiding this Revelation passage. Slavery still exists in the twenty-first century in Africa and other places and is still condoned in Islam; but no Christian group anywhere now fails to condemn it as contrary to the gospel. Even though slavery is plainly described as one of the great evils of the evil city, however, this vision teaches constantly that, slave or free, our souls are either given to God and marked by God as His own or they are sold by the individual to the beast and his minions. Our state in this life, therefore, slave or free, rich or poor, powerful or obscure, does not tell us anything about our eternal destiny with God.

The woman's jewels and fine clothing are now laid waste; seafarers see the smoke of her burning from afar off and lament the demise of their livelihood. But the heavens are rejoicing in her fall; God has finally given judgment against her who seemed so powerful and who was so seductive. Again, her wealth is not evil in itself, for jewels line the streets and gates of heaven in the final visions. What is evil is rebellion against God and leading

---

3. Luke 17:1–2.
4. Rev 18:13.

others by deception into thinking that wealth and power have ultimate value instead of God.

In the fifth vision a mighty angel takes a great millstone and throws it into the sea to symbolize what is happening to Babylon. Remembering the words of Jesus—that for anyone who leads one of these little ones astray, it would be better for him to have a millstone tied around his neck and to be thrown into the sea—we should realize that Babylon doubly deserves this fate because of her leading countless people astray and actually causing many professed Christians, the "little ones," to renounce their faith in order to avoid persecution. In a touching lament, the angel recounts all the beautiful and meaningful details of ordinary life in a city—musicians playing, craftsmen doing their work, lights lit in the evening, wedding feasts, and says that all these will be heard and seen no more. For all nations were deceived by her sorcery, and "in her was found the blood of prophets and of saints, and of all who have been slain on earth."[5] At last, the day of vindication for those martyrs who appeared under the altar has arrived. And every nation is implicated—there is no righteous civil authority, no nation favored by God, which will escape this doom. Unfortunately, the three tapestries illustrating these passages about the destruction of the great whore and the evil city have been lost.

---

5. Rev 18:24.

19

The Tale of Two Cities, or The Harlot and the Bride

THE EVIL CITY HAS been destroyed, and the woman who symbolizes all the evil of that city and all the vanity of human beings who put their trust in wealth, power, and beauty is shown as she really is—not beautiful and desirable but hideous and disgusting, and now, dead. The next vision in this series of seven visions is of the host of heaven rejoicing over her fall. John hears the mighty voice of a great multitude in heaven singing,

> Hallelujah! Salvation and glory and power belong to our God,
> for his judgments are true and just;
> he has judged the great harlot who corrupted the earth with her fornication,
> and he has avenged on her the blood of his servants. . . .
> Hallelujah! The smoke from her goes up forever and ever.
> (Rev 19:1–3)

The tapestry, which had a blue background, is lost, and there is only a photograph of a piece of it. But this fragment is enough to show both the joy in heaven and the fiery bier of the harlot. It shows twelve of the twenty-four elders who cry out, "Amen. Hallelujah," to the heavenly chorus in a cloud. Below them is the head of the harlot as she lies fallen upon the earth with slivers of smoke rising up around her.

We have seen the last of the harlot; it is now time for the showing of the bride in the seventh of this series of visions. Another chorus breaks forth like the sound of many waters, crying,

> "Hallelujah! For the Lord our God the Almighty reigns.
> Let us rejoice and exult and give him the glory,
> for the marriage of the Lamb has come,
> and his bride has made herself ready;
> it was granted her to be clothed with fine linen, bright and pure"—
> for the fine linen is the righteous deeds of the saints.
> (Rev 19:6–8)

Unlike the harlot, who was clothed in purple and scarlet, the bride has fine linen, presumably white, robes which represent the good deeds of all the saints; for the bride of Christ is of course the whole church, all those who have washed their robes in the blood of the Lamb. We remember Jesus's clothing at the transfiguration, whiter than any fuller on earth could bleach them; through his sacrifice, we are given the same pure robes. The beauty of the bride is not because of jewels and a painted face like that of Jezebel as she awaited her death, but rather it is the beauty of the faithful and righteous deeds of all who look to Jesus in hope. The importance of good deeds is again emphasized, not as passports to heaven but as part of the eternal beauty of heaven. That is a big difference!

The angel tells John to write down another benediction: "Blessed are those who are invited to the marriage supper of the Lamb."[1] Fidelity in marriage is the major metaphor of the Hebrew Scriptures for faithfulness to God, and now, in the final book of the Bible, the vision of the eschatological banquet that symbolizes the victory of God over all the forces of rebellion and evil takes up that theme. Using the language of many of the parables of Jesus describing the Kingdom of God as a wedding feast, the Lamb, who gave his life for us out of love, is the eternal bridegroom, and the faithful people of God are both the bride and the guests. The tapestry for this passage is also lost.

John falls down to worship the angel, as he has done earlier, and is given the same admonition—I am only a fellow servant with you; do not worship anyone or anything but God—which is so important to the original hearers and readers of the book. He adds that the angel told him that the testimony of Jesus is the spirit of prophecy, emphasizing his authority to write down this whole vision of prophecy for the whole church to read and be strengthened by. Here we see the angel didactically pointing his finger at John, saying, "Write this." And then we see John trying to fall down at the angel's feet to worship as the angel raises his hand in admonition not to do that.

---

1. Rev 19:9.

The Last Word

Then John sees the heavens opened and the seventh and final series of seven visions begins. They are represented in the sixth set of tapestries, several of which are lost. The first vision is of a white horse with a rider who is called Faithful and True. This marks the reappearance of the conquering rider on the white horse in Rev 6:2, Jesus the Christ; although, as we saw earlier, many interpret that man on a white horse as the first one of a quartet of horsemen sent to bring destruction and warfare, not of Christ. This rider, however, is definitely a representation of Christ the King, victorious in battle over the kingdom of the beast. He both judges and makes war, his eyes are like flame, and he has many crowns upon his head. Most importantly, he has a name inscribed that no one knows but himself, and the name by which he is called is "the Word of God."

We have seen the secret and powerful name of Christ before in this vision; linking it now with the Logos from the prologue of the Gospel of John conveys the mystery of the eternal Christ before all creation—the One though whom all things were made, who yet was born into the world as a little child named Jesus. His robe is dipped in the blood of his foes; yet his armies, the faithful martyrs who follow him on white horses, are arrayed in fine white linen like the bride. The earlier images of the sharp sword in his mouth, the rod of iron with which he rules, and his treading the winepress of the wrath of God reappear here as fulfillment, as with the name inscribed upon his thigh, "King of Kings and Lord of Lords."[2] John is drawing together his themes as he reaches the end of writing down his vision. Christ will conquer, and is even now conquering, no matter what is happening to his faithful people here on earth. The "Hallelujah!" chorus of Handel's *Messiah* has made that inscription "household words" to millions who are not familiar with the Revelation to John at all. As we have seen, it is the tradition to stand for that chorus even in our "post-Christian" age. There is something powerful about these last visions of Christ conquering and God bringing in His kingdom which perhaps stirs even the agnostic soul to stand in hope that it just might be true.

The tapestry for this vision is lost, as is the next one of the birds devouring the impious. The angel calls for the birds that fly in mid-heaven to come for the supper of God. But unlike the marriage supper of the Lamb to which the faithful are invited, this supper is the flesh of the kings, captains, mighty men, and horse and riders, all, both great and small, who still would fight alongside the beast against the conquering might of Christ.

---

2. Rev 19:16.

The deep red background of the next tapestry is very appropriate to depict the battle of the Word of God against the beasts and their mighty men. We see that the many-headed beast and the false prophet, the second beast, are running away in fear as the many-crowned Christ, sword uplifted, gallops towards them on his white horse that looks far more ferocious than the cowering beasts. One of the evil warriors turns to fend off the blow with his scimitar, while three of the blessed warriors follow the Lord into the fray.

The completion of the action is shown next as both the beasts are captured and thrown into the lake of fire that burns with brimstone. Here we see the face of Christ that was hidden by his upraised arm in the previous scene. His many golden and red diadems look like a sultan's turban, and his followers are not shown, emphasizing that the victory over evil is his alone. The beautiful blue background and the lovely green of the grassy field contrast sharply with the gruesome and bloody carnage in the crevice that opens to the lake of fire. Eagles are flying in to do their duty with the bodies of the rest of the slain evil army.

THE TALE OF TWO CITIES, OR THE HARLOT AND THE BRIDE

Their fate reminds one again of the story of Jezebel, whose blood the dogs licked up—these followers of the beast lusted after the harlot, so they suffer a similar fate to that most famous of evil women in the Old Testament. The message is that you get to choose: the beast or the Christ, the false prophet or the true, the harlot or the bride. The followers can surely expect the same fate as the leaders they choose, for eternal ill or eternal blessing.

20

Satan and Christ

THE NEXT FOUR VISIONS in chapter 20 of Revelation focus on the contrast between the eternal fate of Satan and those who are faithful to the Lamb. First, John sees an angel who holds the key to the bottomless pit and a great chain. He seizes "the dragon, that ancient serpent, who is the Devil and Satan"[1] and throws him into the pit, bound for a thousand years. All these titles for the evil one bring together the various stories about him in Scripture, especially the cunning serpent that tempted the first women in the garden of Eden. But the angel says that after the thousand years, he will be loosed again on the world "for a little while." This tapestry has disappeared.

John's next vision is of the thousand-year reign of Christ, when those who had been martyred for the faith come to life and reign with Christ. The rest of the dead do not rise yet. This is the "first resurrection." A beatitude follows for all those who will share in the first resurrection. They are blessed because having died once for the faith, they are immune from the second death, for death has no more power over them. In this tapestry John observes four of these martyrs seated in judgment.

---

1. Rev 20:2.

The traditional interpretation of this reign of a thousand years is that it is not a literal number of years but rather is the time between the first coming of Christ and the second coming. During this time, Christ's reign is a spiritual one in heaven for those who have died confessing the faith, and is evident on earth for the faithful through the church. However, there have always been those who took the number one thousand literally and tried to predict the end of the world by deciding exactly what year it began. When the first millennium approached, many people were prepared for the second coming of Christ. When it did not occur, they had to rethink their literal interpretation of this passage. As the year 2000 approached, again there were sects that believed this was the time foretold in this passage and prepared to meet their Lord, often in very strange and sometimes tragic ways.

The third vision is of the time when the thousand years have ended and Satan is released. One might want to ask the question, "If God is in control, and Christ has conquered and bound Satan, why is Satan ever let loose upon the earth again?" It is hard to understand what this prediction means, except as a way of describing the historical fact that sometimes it

The Last Word

does seem that God is in control and the devil is bound. And yet we know that, as long as we live in this world, times of peace and prosperity do end, sometimes with such ferocity that it seems as if Satan has been let loose on the earth. For Americans who awoke to a lovely fall day on September 11, 2001, it might have seemed that Satan was bound and far away; but suddenly that morning evil was unleashed on the world in new fury hitherto unimaginable. The promise here is that it will only be "for a little while." We know that things sometimes have to get worse before they can get better: John is reminding the faithful that the seeming success of Satan's hideous return really means that the ultimate victory of God is near at hand.

Satan assembles the nations, here called Gog and Magog from the prophecy of Ezekiel about the final assault on Israel, and leads them in a siege on the city beloved of God—that is, the church here on earth. He is depicted here as the beast with seven heads. The beast and the armies of people who are still seduced by him threaten the faithful people inside the walls of the city. Three well-armed warriors valiantly stand outside to defend the city, and at the top of the tapestry we see the fire descending from heaven that will consume the evil ones. God is at last vindicating his elect, once and for all.

God wins! The defeated devil is cast in the lake of fire where the beast and the false prophet were, and they will be tormented forever. All the previous visions of warfare, plague, martyrdoms, demonic beasts, warnings, and lamentation have led to this moment. The battle is over; good has defeated evil once and for all. This tapestry has also been lost.

What remains is to describe the victory in heaven; the sixth vision in this last series is a very dramatic contrast with the last battle scene. John sees God Himself upon a great white throne. Heaven and earth flee away, and all the dead are there standing before the throne. John sees the dead being judged by what is written in books, which presumably contain all their deeds. He also sees the other book, the one that the Lamb was worthy to open, the Book of Life. Then the sea, death, and Hades give up their dead to the judgment. Death and Hades, here personified as forces that were enemies of God, are then thrown into the lake of fire with the devil. Death came into the world in the garden of Eden because of human sin. If there were no death, there would be no need for a place of the dead, or Hades. They now are destroyed since there is no more room for them in the new heaven and new earth where sin cannot enter in. Anyone whose name is not found in the Book of Life is also cast into the lake of fire. There are no gradations of Hell here, such as are later developed in literature like Dante's *Inferno*. The choice is simple: those who follow the evil one get to join him for eternity. Those who choose God get to join him.

As we have already observed in earlier passages, a statement that each one is judged according to his deeds is disturbing to many Christians who see this passage in conflict with Saint Paul's teachings on salvation solely through faith in Christ, not through good works. That is a perennial problem in Christian theology—deciding just what it means to be saved through faith over against being judged according to one's deeds. But the book of Revelation is not teaching that one can earn one's way to heaven by doing the required number of righteous deeds. The saints in heaven are clearly described as those who have washed their robes in the blood of the Lamb. Their faith in the saving grace of Jesus's sacrifice on the cross has made them fit for heaven.

The meaning here of being judged by one's deeds is that one's righteous deeds have eternal significance. They follow us and become the jewels in our crown, whereas our sinful deeds are washed away by the blood of Christ. The faithful are then given the white robe and the crown, not on their own merit but rather through their faith in the One who is worthy, the Lamb That Was Slain. The names written in the Book of Life are the names of those who have been faithful to Christ; having one's name written in that book is what saves one from the lake of fire. The choice which has eternal consequences is the choice of whether or not to follow Jesus and put all one's trust not "in our own righteousness but in [his] manifold and great mercy," as the Book of Common Prayer puts it.[2]

This tapestry is also missing; it is a very great loss, for the theme of the last judgment inspired some of the greatest works of medieval and Renaissance art. It would be fascinating to see how Jean de Bruges conceived of it and how it fit into the wonderful iconography of these tapestries.

---

2. Episcopal Church, Book of Common Prayer, 337.

21

The New Jerusalem, the Bride of Christ

> Then I saw a new heaven and a new earth; for the first heaven and the first earth had passed away, and the sea was no more. (Rev 21:1)

JOHN'S REVELATION IS NOW nearing fulfillment; in the seventh vision of this seventh series of visions, he actually sees what Jesus has promised and what the ancient prophets have foretold—a new heaven and a new earth. The perfect number of seven, as we have seen, is a unifying theme throughout this book, conveying the idea of wholeness and perfection. At last, we have reached the infinite number, seven times seven, and the final vision of eternity in the presence of God.

Now one may ask, "Why do we need a new heaven? What's wrong with the old one?" The answer lies in two ideas. First, "the heavens and the earth" is the Hebrew way of describing all of creation, as in the first chapter of Genesis: "In the beginning, God created the heavens and the earth."[1] The heavens are the location of the sun and moon and stars and also the domain of the flying birds. What God has created, and what human beings have sullied with our disobedience, will now be recreated. The second idea is that the old heaven, taken as the dwelling place of God, could not be a perfect place until after all these struggles documented in this vision, like the rebellion against God in Rev 12, have taken place. Great portents appeared in heaven: the woman clothed with the sun but also the great red dragon

---

1. Gen 1:1.

that sought to destroy her and her child. Then there arose war in heaven: Michael and his angels fighting against the dragon, which was defeated and thrown down.

A new heaven, therefore, as well as a new earth, is promised to the faithful at the end of time when the petition of our Lord that God's will be done on earth as in heaven will be perfectly fulfilled. The voice from heaven goes on to proclaim that from now on the dwelling place of God is with men. "He will dwell with them and they shall be his people, and God himself will be with them."[2] So it seems that the new heaven and the new earth are essentially the same place, since God and human beings are at last dwelling together. They are not in some always-perfect place where God sits unchanged throughout eternity. Instead, the consummation of God's loving creation of the whole world is finally achieved through the obedience of the Lamb That Was Slain, uniting God and the men and women he created in his image and likeness in this new creation.

It is very significant that the new heaven is called a city, the new Jerusalem, which John sees coming down from heaven from God, "Prepared as a bride adorned for her husband."[3] There is no idealizing of nature "unspoiled" by human beings in this vision. Deep within our hearts we know we cannot go back to the idyllic state of Eden, loaded as we are with all the weight of human history, nor should we desire to do so. We are meant to be together, not alone, and the place where human beings live together is called a city. But God will dwell with us there, just as He was wont to walk in the garden of Eden in the cool of the day.

And love is the theme—love like that of a husband and wife who have freely chosen to be with each other for ever. The new city is dressed as a pure bride, the antithesis of the evil city of Babylon depicted as a whore or harlot. Whereas the harlot represented those who trusted in the powers of this world, the new and eternal city of Jerusalem, the bride, represents the church—all those who have been faithful to Christ in spite of terrible persecutions by the rulers of this world and the seductive powers of the harlot and the beasts.

The rest of this chapter is a detailed description of the walls, streets, gates, and trees of the heavenly city. It will have a river flowing through it, and the architecture and cultivated garden forever ennobles all that is beautiful and worthy of the work of human hands. The voice continues,

---

2. Rev 21:3.
3. Rev 21:2.

promising comfort to all the inhabitants of the eternal city in words echoing those of Isa 25:8, "He will wipe away every tear from their eyes, and death shall be no more, neither shall there be mourning nor crying not pain any more, for the former things have passed away."[4] How many times have these words been read at funerals, and how many times has this promise brought comfort to those who are bereaved and suffering! The confident vision that there will be a place where God will dwell with His people and comfort us and heal us, no matter how difficult or painful our lot is now upon this earth, is the essence of the Revelation to John. This is one of the reasons that this book of the Bible, strange as it is, has always been so beloved by faithful people.

In the tapestry John is shown gazing at the vision of the new Jerusalem floating in heaven, with the blue background all around it and the sea beneath it. God himself is speaking to him marvelous words of comfort and encouragement. "Behold, I make all things new," he continues, promising an eternal newness in which things do not grow old or worn or diminished in their timeless perfection. "He who sat upon the throne" then says,

> Behold I make all things new. . . . Write this, for these words are trustworthy and true . . . It is done! I am the Alpha and the Omega, the beginning and the end. To the thirsty I will give water without price from the fountain of the water of life. He who conquers shall have this heritage, and I will be his God and he shall be my son. (Rev 21:5–7)

---

4. Rev 21:4.

This promise echoes Isaiah's prophecy, "Ho! Everyone that thirsts, come to the waters; and he who has no money, come, buy and eat! Come, buy wine and milk without money and without price."[5] It is also the life-giving water freely available to all that Jesus promised to the woman at the well in John's Gospel: "The water that I shall give him will become in him a spring of water welling up to eternal life."[6] And best of all, to the one who conquers—that is, who is faithful under persecution and temptation—God promises a heritage as His son or daughter.

These assurances are followed by an admonition for all who might be considering apostasy: cowards, the faithless or polluted, murderers, fornicators, sorcerers, idolaters, and liars—in other words, those who worshiped the beasts and were seduced by the harlot. They will be consigned to the lake of fire that is the second death into which we saw the devil thrown forever in Rev 20. Reiterating this judgment seems harsh here in this final vision of joy, but we must remember that John is hoping to encourage fidelity by using both the carrot and the stick, as the saying goes. It also brings to mind the passage in the peaceful Twenty-Third Psalm: "Thou preparest a table before me in the presence of mine enemies."[7] The victory of the faithful necessarily means that the tormentors will be defeated. As Saint Thomas

---

5. Isa 55:1.
6. John 4:14.
7. Ps 23:5 KJV.

THE NEW JERUSALEM, THE BRIDE OF CHRIST

concluded, evil is not some *thing*, but it is real. Since it is real it must be destroyed for pure goodness to reign.

The linking of the destruction of evil with the triumph of good is again emphasized, for it is the angel who had the seven bowls of the seven last plagues who speaks now to John, carrying him away in the Spirit to a great, high mountain to show him the new Jerusalem. The detailed description of the city echoes the description of the new temple given in a vision to the prophet Ezekiel. But this passage is strictly a symbolic description; its measurements, which are all multiples of the perfect number twelve, represent the twelve tribes of Israel and the twelve apostles and cannot be used to construct anything. These are intellectual and emotional images, as so many of the descriptions in this vision are—a gate made out of a pearl or gold which is "clear as glass"—although they have inspired countless graphic artists to attempt to depict them. It is interesting that Jean de Bruges did not make the attempt to portray these details in the tapestries. This next tapestry shows the angel with the measuring rod of gold in one hand and holding John's hand in the other as he shows him the eternal city, the bride of Christ. The city is seen only from the outside. The angel's wings dominate the scene, and one wing seems to be extending its protection over the city walls.

Genesis teaches that work is part of God's plan for us in the creation; God put the first man in the garden to work, to till it and to keep it. Now

Revelation completes that theme by teaching that our work has eternal significance. All the most beautiful things of this earth that are found or mined and then shaped and polished by human labor are the building materials of this city. The foundations are of jasper, crystal, sapphire, agate, emerald, onyx, carnelian, topaz, chrysoprase, jacinth, amethyst; the gates are of pearls, and the streets are paved with gold. The richness and beauty of these precious jewels and metals symbolize the best of the creation brought to completion by human effort. Without work, inventiveness, and desire to fashion things of beauty from the natural world, we would not have jewelry or vessels of gold or art and architecture at all. The eternal city thus represents the purpose of God's good creation; it is to be shaped and hammered by the people He has made in His image and whom He blessed with skill and diligence.

In God's new heaven and new earth, He makes room for the labor and good works of our lives, which are the stars in our eternal crowns. As Canon Fenton put it, all the work we have done out of love and with true diligence will be there, not as it actually turned out in this life with all our imperfections, but as we meant it to be. The books we wrote, the surgical operations we performed, the lessons we taught, the houses we cleaned, the visits we paid to the sick, the children we raised, the trials we won, the accounts we kept, the fields we plowed and planted, the sermons we preached, the meals we cooked and served, and so on and so forth, will be transformed by our loving Father into what they were supposed to be, unmarred by our failings. To receive praise and honor for what we have done well with a whole heart is what it means to be blessed; and "blessed are those who are invited to the marriage supper of the Lamb."[8]

In contrast to the vision of the new temple given to Ezekiel in exile, this vision of the completion of all things is without a temple, for in the presence of God no further sacrifice is needed or appropriate. Beholding the face of the Lord God Almighty and the Lamb will be the culmination of joy and the perfection of desire. Furthermore, there will be no heavenly bodies in the new heaven, for it has no need of sun or moon to shine and give it light. "The glory of God is its light and its lamp is the Lamb."[9] And since "time shall be no more,"[10] there is no need for the sun and the moon to regulate days and weeks and years, as Genesis tells us they were created to do.

---

8. Rev 19:9.

9. Rev 21:23.

10. As in the James Black hymn, "When the Roll Is Called Up Yonder."

And now all the nations and kings of the earth shall walk in this light and bring their glory and honor into the city. This is an amazing claim: those who were deceived by the harlot and the beast will at last see the light and walk into the city whose gates will never be shut and where there will be no day or night. These lines represent the fulfillment of the prophecy of Isaiah:

> And nations shall come to your light
> And kings to the brightness of your rising....
> Your gates shall be open continually;
> day and night they shall not be shut;
> that men may bring to you the wealth of nations,
> with their kings led in procession.
> (Isa 60:3, 11)

Some interpreters think that John quotes Isaiah here without realizing how it seems to contradict the previous vision of the destruction of the wicked. Lending support to that view, the final admonition in this chapter does reiterate that the unclean and those who commit abominations or falsehoods will not enter, but only those whose names are written in the Lamb's Book of Life. But perhaps this last vision of Revelation is telling us that, in the end, it is just possible that no one will be able to resist God's love and grace and the beauty of that light. If the kings of the earth are welcome, then no one need despair. The crucial decision is recognizing that the Lamb is King of Kings and Lord of Lords. The Lord God does not desire the death of sinners but rather that they turn from their wickedness and live, as Ezekiel wrote. So, the kings of this earth, whoever those kings may be in any time and place, if they heed the warnings of this vision and turn from their wickedness, may enter the city and live. As Ps 138:4 puts it, "All the kings of the earth shall praise thee, O Lord, for they have heard the words of thy mouth."

22

Come, Lord Jesus!

THE BEGINNING OF THE last chapter of Revelation is a continuation of the description of the Holy City, the new Jerusalem. But now we see familiar aspects of the original garden of Eden, which the Lord God made and planted and into which he put the first human beings. The new Jerusalem is a culmination of the work of human hands and, at the same time, a restoration of elements of that place of original blessedness. It has flowing water and trees that represent life and knowledge.

The angel shows John "the river of the water of life, bright as crystal, flowing from the throne of God and of the Lamb,"[1] as described in Ps 46:4: "There is a river whose streams make glad the city of God, the holy habitation of the Most High." There is only one throne; God and the Lamb are both there. In the last tapestry that survives, the figure of God upon the throne looks very like the earlier representation of Jesus in the third tapestry, but the Lamb is shown at His right side astride the rainbow, forefeet upon the lap of God. The whole world is represented as a golden orb under His feet. John has his hands folded together in an attitude of praise and adoration. The trees for the healing of nations are depicted also, as well as three faithful souls joining John in adoration of the living God.

---

1. Rev 22:1.

The water which flows is a symbol of the water which, mixed with blood, flowed from the wounded side of Jesus on the cross, as well as recalling the water from the rivers that flowed in Eden. It is the living water which assuages all thirst, which cleanses and refreshes, and which is free to all who seek it. The fathers of the church taught that this water also represents the Holy Spirit, which flows eternally from God to renew His creation in the waters of baptism. The waters of Heaven nourish the tree of life which bears twelve kinds of fruit, one for each month. In the first Psalm the righteous man is said to be "like a tree planted by the streams of water, that yields its fruit in its season, and its leaf does not wither. In all that he does he prospers."[2] For a Christian, this is a prefiguring of Christ, the one truly righteous man. Since this "tree" grows on either side of the river, perhaps this is supposed to mean twelve different trees, each with a different fruit for its season. But whatever the number of trees, all of their leaves are for the healing of nations. Now "the nations" in the Bible always refers to other nations, not Israel. Since the new Israel is now the church, the company of faithful people who are safe within the city, "the nations" must refer to others who are still outside but who will come to be healed.

Never before in the Bible has a tree been described as having the properties of healing. There are healing herbs and leaves for medicinal purposes but not trees or any other plant for the healing of the state of sin in the world. God is called the one "who heals all your diseases" in Ps 103:3, and a

2. Ps 1:3.

major sign that Jesus is the Messiah is his power to heal, as was foretold by the prophets. In the Gospels Jesus often heals people out of compassion but calls attention to the healing as a sign of the coming kingdom of God. In the new heaven and the new earth, the trees themselves will have the power to heal sinful nations who have not recognized that the Lord is the only God, and who are themselves scarred and wounded by the evil they inflict on other nations. One thinks today of the seemingly intractable conflict between many Muslim Arab nations and the Jewish state of Israel, and the hatred that some nations have for the United States of America, and longs anew for the healing of the nations that only God can give.

These healing leaves are another indication that this vision ends with the hope that all nations and peoples actually can be healed, that it is God's intention to do so in His own good time according to His plan. The next verse, "Then there shall no more be anything accursed,"[3] further gives us reason to hope that, in the end, no one will be able to withstand the burning love of God.

The reappearance of the tree of life from Eden is also very important. Remember that God expels the man and the woman from the garden to keep them away from the tree of life once they have eaten of the tree of the knowledge of good and evil, "Lest he put forth his hand and take also of the tree of life, and eat, and live forever."[4] God places the cherubim and a flaming sword to guard the way to the tree of life.[5] All the imagery of Eden and original blessedness is recapitulated here in the final scene of the vision. God himself is showing John the way to eternal blessedness. It cannot be a return to Eden; that is a vain hope. Rather God Himself came to us, as one of us, to show the way to his marriage feast. It is only because of the sacrificial death of the Lamb, and through faith in His blood, that we are able to follow Him through persecution and trials, confident in our hope that life and joy await us in the presence of the Lord. We will find life eternal there where the tree of life is waiting for us.

Then the greatest joy of the servants of God will be that, since His name will be there upon their foreheads forever, they can worship Him and see his face. The tradition throughout the Bible is that no one can see God face-to-face and live. Moses did, but then he had to veil his face from the people for it shone so brightly with reflected glory. Saint Paul foresaw that "now we see

---

3. Rev 22:3.
4. Gen 3:22.
5. Gen 3:24.

in a mirror dimly, but then face to face."⁶ Here that hope is fulfilled. Seeing God face-to-face does not bring death but instead is the reward of eternal life with Him. "Beloved, we are God's children now; it does not yet appear what we shall be, but we know that when he appears we shall be like him, for we shall see him as he is."⁷

John says again that this glory of God will be the only light of the heavenly city—there will be no need for any created light, whether it be the sun or a lamp. Here again he is speaking of the fulfillment of the prophecy of Isaiah:

> The sun shall be no more
> your light by day,
> nor for brightness shall the moon
> give light to you by night;
> but the LORD will be your everlasting light.
> (Isa 60:19)

Jesus at the transfiguration shone with a foretaste of his resurrected glory as well as with trails of his former glory, his true glory as the Second Person of the Trinity. In Heaven his glory is completely revealed, so the Lamb is the light of the city of God. And finally the saints, who are shown in this tapestry facing God and worshiping Him, will reign with the Lamb and the Lord God forever and ever.

That is the end of the last vision of the Revelation. What remains is for John to attest to the veracity of his words and to ensure that they belong with the rest of the sacred writings in which God speaks to His people. As we said at the beginning, the purpose of this revelation is to answer the question "Where is Jesus now?" and its corollary, "If Jesus is the Son of God and Lord, then why are his people suffering so terribly? Why does he not return now and vindicate us?" These questions have now been answered for those who listen with ears of faith. John says that Jesus himself tells him that God sent the angel to show John what "must take place"—the sense of urgency and immediacy never fades—and promises, "These words are trustworthy and true. . . . Behold, I am coming soon."⁸ He pronounces a blessing again on all who keep the prophecy of the book—that means, those who believe it and order their lives by it. John, calling himself by name as he did in the beginning, vows that he really saw and heard these

---

6. 1 Cor 13:12.
7. 1 John 3:2.
8. Rev 22:6–7.

things. Whoever this man named John is, he wants us all to know his name and to remember that he is one of us, a follower of Christ.

In the last fragments of the tapestries, we see John kneeling before the angel, who tells him again not to worship him but to worship only God. The tapestry of John and the angel we have seen before is included here because it illustrates the same themes. The temptation to give in and worship the emperor in order to get along in the Roman Empire was so great that this lesson is repeated several times—do not worship anyone but God, not even His angel. In the other fragment the angel is telling him not to seal up the book because the time of its fulfillment is near. This directive is the opposite of the admonition in the book of Daniel, from whom John takes so much of his themes and imagery:

> But you, Daniel, shut up the words, and seal the book, until the time of the end. . . . Go your way, Daniel, for the words are shut up and sealed until the time of the end. . . . Blessed is he who waits and comes to the thousand three hundred and thirty-five days. (Dan 12:4, 9, 12)

One reason given for Daniel's being told to seal up the words of the book is that it was actually written much later than the historical time in which it was set, and was attributed to the legendary hero Daniel to give it authority. In order to make it seem that Daniel had written it, and that it was just discovered, the author says that the angel told Daniel to seal it up until the end. John, however, is given the opposite command. He is writing what he has seen for his fellow Christians to read *now*, and he believes his message is clear that the coming of the Lord will be soon. But he adds, realistically, that life will go on until that moment, with the evildoer still doing evil and the holy still being holy, side by side, as in the parable of the wheat and the tares awaiting the harvest in the Gospel parable.

Now Jesus himself speaks to John again with a clear message: "Behold I am coming soon, bringing my recompense, to repay everyone for what he has done,"[9] sounding again the theme of the eternal significance of our actions. In this final message Jesus uses the appellation for himself that God the Father has used twice before in this vision: "I am the Alpha and the Omega, the first and the last, the beginning and the end."[10] This is the final point of the book—that Jesus who died for our sins is in fact God. As the prologue to the Gospel of John makes clear, the Word is one with the Father from the beginning and is the One through whom all things were made.

The seventh and final blessing of the book is,

> Blessed are those who wash their robes, that they may have the right to the tree of life and that they may enter the city by the gates. (Rev 22:14)

Outside are the dogs, sorcerers, fornicators, murderers, and everyone who loves and practices falsehood. One wonders why dogs are the only animals said to be outside for eternity; many of us cannot think of any animal less deserving of such punishment, and all the creatures God made are called "very good" in Genesis. But "dogs" is a metaphor in Scripture for those who willfully defy God. Speaking falsehood, deliberately following a lie, and building one's life upon that lie are the ultimate rejection of God and of His Christ, who is "the way, the *truth*, and the life."[11]

Jesus ends the vision as he began, with the reminder that this message is for the churches; it is not the kind of writing that would be readily understood by anyone outside of a believing community. It is not Christian apologetics

---

9. Rev 22:12.
10. Rev 22:13.
11. John 14:6; emphasis added.

The Last Word

or evangelism; it is for the encouragement of those who already bear the seal of Christ. Jesus here calls himself "the bright morning star" and "the root and offspring of David,"[12] recalling his earlier epithets in the message to the seven churches which began this book, coming full circle, as it were. "The Spirit and the Bride say 'Come.' And let him who hears say, 'Come.'"[13] The Holy Spirit, who has caught John up into this vision, the bride that is the whole company of blessed people in the heavenly city, and the church still on earth long for the fulfillment of this prophecy.

12. Rev 22:16.
13. Rev 22:17.

John speaks in warning to anyone who hears and read this book. No one is to add or take away from the words; it is not for other Christians to edit. They can struggle to understand it, as millions of Christians have endeavored to do throughout the centuries. But the greatest hubris of all is to think that anyone, no matter how brilliant a scholar or how holy a saint, is entitled to rewrite the words of Scripture. In our own day, those with a specific "good" agenda often do just that. It makes one wonder what we would have left of the word of God if translators in every age had felt free to alter the words to suit the times. Interpreting them anew is the task of every generation, of course, but that is quite different from rewriting and editing them. Although "new occasions teach new duties, / time makes ancient good uncouth, / They must onward still and upward, / who would keep abreast of truth,"[14] as James Russell Lowell wrote, John is reminding us that the word of God is not to be altered to suit our sensitivities and taste but is there to challenge us anew in every time and place. What would be left to correct us and to call us to repentance if we have repeatedly remade the word of God into our own "enlightened" image?

> He who testifies to these things says, "Surely I am coming soon." Amen. Come, Lord Jesus! The grace of the Lord Jesus be with all the saints. Amen. (Rev 22:20–21)

The book ends with another assurance from Jesus, testifying to the truth of the vision and reiterating the promise made therein. The response John gives fittingly ends all of the Bible: "Amen. Come, Lord Jesus!" This was the fervent prayer of all early Christians; Saint Paul uses it in the Aramaic form in 1 Corinthians, *Maranatha*. It is another way of saying, as we do in the prayer Jesus taught us, "Thy kingdom come." We have said that the whole Revelation to John can be interpreted as an elaboration on the Lord's Prayer; it ends as it begins, with the prayer for Jesus to come, "For thine is the kingdom."

---

14. Lowell, "Once to Every Man and Nation," stanza 3.

Conclusion

THE LAST BOOK OF the Bible ends with the prayer of the faithful and with a benediction such as the church always offers the faithful at their parting: "The grace of the Lord Jesus Christ be with all the saints. Amen."[1] The tapestries of Angers speak to us of the longing of those Christians centuries ago for the coming kingdom and their desire "to be in that number when the saints go marching in." We have the same longing today as they did, along with the original hearers of this vision and all the faithful people who have found hope in it ever since. Our lives are sometimes overwhelmed with evil from without and from within. The book of Revelation assures us that God is ultimately in control and that Jesus is truly our savior. He will save us if we put our trust in him and not in the works of our hands or the cleverness of our minds. He will save us from our sins if we bring our robes to be washed in his blood. He will vanquish the powers of evil which seduce and deceive us, no matter how powerful they appear to be at any time.

Furthermore, when we gather together in His name in our churches, we know that God's messenger angel is watching over us and will bring us God's guidance. Together and privately, we should be constant in prayer because our prayers are part of God's purpose for the world, rising to His presence with the incense from the heavenly altar and actually becoming a part of His mighty deeds. And our good deeds have significance for all eternity; they too are part of God's plan and purpose for this world He has made. They are not a way to build up merit to have a right to enter Heaven, for Jesus, the Lamb That Was Slain, is the only worthy one, and his righteousness is both necessary and sufficient for all of us. But everything that is good is a part of God's will, and God will perfect our imperfect human goodness and use it as part of the beauty of Heaven. God created us out of love, and in the end, He invites those who choose to be with Him into the

---

1. Rev 22:21.

CONCLUSION

joy of His presence. There, like a bride greeting her beloved husband, we will enter into the joy of Heaven at the wedding feast of the Lamb.

These are comforting words and good words with which to end all of Sacred Scripture. Throughout every time, in every place, in every trial and temptation, in every joy and delight, may the grace of our Lord Jesus Christ be with you. Amen.

Bibliography

Alexander, Frances Cecil. "He Is Risen, He Is Risen!" #180 in *The Episcopal Hymnal 1982*. New York: Church Hymnal, 1985. https://hymnary.org/hymn/EH1982/180.

Browning, Robert. *Pippa Passes*. New York: Doubleday, 1909.

Cross, Bryan. "St. Irenaeus's Testimony to the Apostles." Lonely Pilgrim, June 28, 2013. https://lonelypilgrim.com/2013/06/28/st-irenaeus-testimony-to-the-apostles/.

Donne, John. "A Lecture upon the Shadow." Poetry Foundation. https://www.poetryfoundation.org/poems/44118/a-lecture-upon-the-shadow.

Episcopal Church. The Book of Common Prayer. New York: Church Publishing, 1979.

Harmon, Nolan B., et al., eds. "James, Peter, John, Jude, Revelation." Vol. 12 of *The Interpreter's Bible*. New York: Abingdon, 1957.

Heber, Reginald. "Holy, Holy, Holy." #362 in *The Episcopal Hymnal 1982*. New York: Church Hymnal, 1985. https://hymnary.org/hymn/EH1982/362.

Lewis, C. S. *Letters to Malcolm: Chiefly on Prayer*. San Diego, CA: Harvest, 1964.

Lowell, James Russell. "Once to Every Man and Nation." #519 in *The Hymnal of the Protestant Episcopal Church*. New York: Church Pension Fund, 1940.

May, Herbert G., and Bruce M. Metzger. *The New Oxford Annotated Bible with the Apocrypha: Revised Standard Version*. New York: Oxford University Press, 1977.

Muel, Francis, et al. *La Tenture de l'Apocalypse d'Angers*. Nantes: L'Association pour le développement de l'Inventaire Général des Monuments et des Richesses Artistiques en Région des Pays de la Loire, 1987.

Origen. *The Commentary on the Gospel of John*. Translated by Allan Menzies. In vol. 9 of *The Ante-Nicene Fathers*. Edited by Allan Menzies. Buffalo, NY: Christian Literature, 1896. Revised and edited for New Advent by Kevin Knight. https://www.newadvent.org/fathers/101505.htm.

Percy, William Alexander. "They Cast Their Nets in Galilee." #661 in *The Episcopal Hymnal 1982*. New York: Church Hymnal, 1985. https://hymnary.org/hymn/EH1982/661.

Phillips, J. B. *The Book of Revelation: A New Translation*. London: Bles, 1957.

Shakespeare, William. *Hamlet*. Edited by Ada S. Ambler et al. London: Blackie & Son, 1902.

———. *The Tragedie of Macbeth*. Edited by Mark Harvey Liddell. New York: Doubleday, 1903.

Stone, Samuel John. "The Church's One Foundation." #525 in *The Episcopal Hymnal 1982*. New York: Church Hymnal, 1985. https://hymnary.org/hymn/EH1982/525.

www.ingramcontent.com/pod-product-compliance
Lightning Source LLC
Chambersburg PA
CBHW070333230426
43663CB00011B/2300